"Bullet Hole of the Year Award....The best crime series in years, this one had intelligent scripts." —**TV Guide**

"The best show on prime-time network television..." —**Associated Press**

"**Wiseguy** succeeds on solid plotting, crisp and tough writing and vivid performances led by Ken Wahl." —**USA Today**

"The most exciting, the most credible and, above all, the most literate crime drama to surface on television in quite some time...The triumph of **Wiseguy** is that it's an action show where the most exciting conflicts are psychological...It's more than a series. It's a necessity."—**New York Newsday**

"The season had one bull's eye, if not in the ratings then definitely in dramatic impact. CBS' **Wiseguy** had the craziest charge of endangerment since the hallelujah days of *Hill Street Blues*. **Wiseguy** customized the role of Steelgrave for (Ray) Sharkey, and he in turn whipped it into a souped-up comeback vehicle. (Kevin) Spacey did stuff I've never seen anyone do on TV before...The real excitement, as **Wiseguy** proved, is where the balcony tilts toward the crazed, lavish skyline. Top of the world!" —**Vanity Fair**

"**Wiseguy** has the straightforward rambunctiousness of the best American entertainment; it's a big, stylish vehicle with a full-sized V-8 engine. This sleek sucker buzzes down the freeway so fast that you barely have time to register all of the ideas—good and bad—that come as optional equipment, mounted on the polished wood dashboard...in addition to the skillful interweaving of serial elements, **Wiseguy** has a sweaty manliness that's self-deprecating and unselfconsciously slick." —**Rolling Stone**

"**Wiseguy** which featured the best action-drama writing of the year (and probably the best acting job by guest Ray Sharkey, of any series on the air this season), suggests it has the potential to be a big-number action hit." —**Weekly Variety**

"Wahl brings an uncanny commitment to the part. It's no wonder the crooks are fooled. His stance, his glare, his accent, speak of an upbringing on the stoops and in the streets....The strength of the show lies in its characterization. **Wiseguy** is people rich. Cops and crooks are drawn in three full dimensions."

—**San Francisco Examiner**

"Vinnie, the main character of the CBS dramatic series **Wiseguy**, has developed into one of the most complex protagonists on television." —**Houston Chronicle**

"**Wiseguy** is slickly produced, well plotted and well acted....It tries to look serious and sinister—and it succeeds." —**People Magazine**

"Welcome to television's darkest, most complex, humane treatment of crime and law enforcement. **Wiseguy** is one of the most complex, realistic under̶ stories on TV."—**Denver Post**

"If there's a word that describes **Wiseguy**, it's involvii͟ plex world and keeps your attention. That's what a going to make you forego renting a tape for the nigh͟

...̶gton **Post Syndicate**

EDITED

AND

DESIGNED

BY

HAL

SCHUSTER

THE UNOFFICIAL STORY OF THE MAKING OF A WISEGUY

By Edward Gross

PIONEER BOOKS, INC.   LAS VEGAS, NEVADA

Library of Congress Cataloging-in-Publication Data
Gross, Edward   1960—
    The Unofficial Story of the Making of a Wiseguy

    1. Wiseguy (Television program) I. Title
ISBN 1-55698-256-9

Published by Pioneer Books, Inc., 5715 N. Balsam Rd., Las Vegas, NV, 89130.
International Standard Book Number: 1-55698-256-9

First Printing 1990

To the cast and crew of WISEGUY
Thanks for making television fun again

ACKNOWLEDGEMENTS:

There is no doubt in my mind that **Secret File: The Unofficial Making of a Wiseguy** would not have been possible without the cooperation of a wide variety of people, and to them I am extremely indebted. For taking the time to be interviewed, I'd like to thank Jonathan Banks, Jim Byrnes, Ray Sharkey, Ron Silver, Dennis Lipscomb, Paul Guilfoyle, Stanely Tucci, Eric Blakeney (who I thank twice—and he knows why), Stephen Kronish, Les Sheldon, John Schulian, Frank Lupo, Robert Iscove, Lyndon Chubbock, Larry Shaw and a very special thanks to David Burke. In addition, my appreciation to the various publicists who arranged these interviews, my friends Michael Lepper and Paul Nicosia, who got me hooked on the damn show in the first place; my wife, Eileen, for listening to me rant and rave about this book for so long, and for dealing with my zealousness everytime I got another interview; my baby son, Teddy, for not eating my **Wiseguy** tapes and assorted friends who shared my enthusiasm for the series, including Dexter Frank, Tom Sanders, Eric Allen, John Shahinian, Hal Schuster, Mark Altman and Lisa Jacobson.

CONTENTS

INTRODUCTION

I refused to watch it.

Plain and simple.

It was a point I'd made clear to everyone. Sorry, fellows, I would respond, it's not my cup of tea. Is there any science fiction? Is there any fantasy? Are there some good laughs? No? Then why should I bother? After all, I've never been much of a fan of television crime shows, because they've never been able to match the scale of such big screen action fare as James Bond or *Lethal Weapon*. But each week, like clockwork, Paul and Mike would corner me at the office, and launch their double-barreled assault: "Did you watch it yet?"

"Listen guys," I would patiently explain for the umpteenth time, "I don't watch **Wiseguy**. Why don't you hassle somebody who does?"

They never stopped asking, and I'm grateful for it.

Somehow I had made it through the entire 1987-88 television season without viewing a single episode, but when CBS began re-airing the Sonny Steelgrave arc during the summer of '88, I found that I had no choice. The persistent duo would never leave me in peace until I watched at least one episode, so I thought I would placate them, and where better to start than with the two hour pilot that launched the series?

"Look," I remember saying, "I'm going to make your day. I'm going to watch **Wiseguy** tonight. In fact, I'm going to tape it, this way if you ask me if I've seen an episode ten years from now, I'll be able to whip out my tape and say 'yes.' Happy now?"

The triumphant smiles that crossed their lips are the things that wanted posters are made of. Their reaction was also kind of smug, as though they were privately saying, "Gotcha!"

They were right.

I watched and taped the pilot, and was blown away by it. I was stunned by the instant rapport between Ken Wahl and Ray Sharkey, as well as the production values of the show itself. Quite simply, this was unlike any other crime series I had ever seen, and I eagerly looked forward to the next episode and the next and the next....until it was time for OCB officer Vinnie Terranova to move on to his next undercover investigation. Sonny was gone, but Mel and Susan Profitt quickly took his place. Yet I was feeling frustrated. The second arc would span approximately ten episodes, I was told, and that meant ten more long and drawn out weeks before I knew how it all ended and season two began.

Then my friend John gave me videocassettes of the entire Profitt arc, which I watched in a single weekend.

It was too late. I was infected by *Wiseguymania*. I needed a fix...badly. But it was still a month before the second season began. What was I to do? My eyes wandered towards my videocassette collection and the tapes labeled Sonny Steelgrave. "What the hell," I thought, "I'll watch 'em again," and that's exactly what I did.

What, you may be wondering, does all of this have to do with the volume you hold in your hand. Simply put, you just don't watch **Wiseguy** casually. It becomes an obsession that grips you with such fervor that you want to spread the disease. You discuss the show just enough to get the unwashed tentatively interested, then you loan out copies (never the originals) of your episodes and—bam!—they're hopelessly hooked. It happened with three other friends, Dexter, Tom and Pioneer Books publisher Hal Schuster. Now the legion is growing, and there's nothing wrong with that.

Secret File: The Unofficial Making of a Wiseguy serves as testament to the creative effort made by the cast and crew that has resulted in one of the freshest television series to arrive in quite a few years. Personally speaking, the most exciting aspect of writing this text was the way that those who have labored on the show were willing to discuss the series in minute detail, taking time from their very busy schedules to set the record straight. They are justifiably proud of their accomplishments, doing their share to help elevate the medium.

I thank each and every one of them for the pleasure they've brought forth and the aid they've provided me. May we continue to thrill to the adventures of Vinnie Terranova, Frank McPike and Lifeguard for years to come.

Edward Gross

December, 1989

THE BEGINNINGS

Innovative. Intelligent. Unpredictable.

These are words that come to mind when discussing **Wiseguy**, and for good reason. The CBS series, in the midst of its third season at the time of this writing, is doing its bit to revolutionize the medium, transforming episodic television into something along the rather paradoxical lines of an anthology with continuing characters.

The show's premise is simple. The execution of it is not. Ken Wahl portrays OCB (Organized Crime Bureau) agent Vincent Terranova, who's spent 18 months in prison to help create his cover as a "wise-guy." Upon his release, he begins a series of undercover investigations which have involved him with a variety of society's undesirables, ranging from the mob to white supremacists, from international arms dealers to ruthless music industry power brokers. The difference between this show and every other cop series is that the characters deliver a visceral quality not usually found on the tube. Whether you're talking about Terranova, his field director Frank McPike or Lifeguard, the behind the scenes operator who has saved Vinnie on more than a couple of occasions, realism is the name of the game. In addition, the villains aren't dispatched after one or two episodes. In fact, there have been instances where it's taken nine installments of a **Wiseguy** saga—or arc, as it is referrred to by the show's creative team—for a tale to be resolved. In addition, there isn't always a clear-cut separation between good and evil, and there have been moments when the audience could well have wondered which side of the fence Terranova would ultimately land on.

"That's the whole point to the series," actor Ken Wahl once explained, "to show that everybody's not all good, not all bad. These things intertwine, and therein lies the conflict."

"In the beginning" states co-executive producer Les Sheldon, "a lot of people thought we were doing a mob show, but found out real quick that we weren't. The idea of the show is to kind of do it as an anthology, but string it together with this guy as he runs into these different types of human beings and peels away at them. The result is that we, through him, find out who they are and not just what they are. Because of that, he has some tremendous conflicts going on inside, and—right, wrong or indifferent—he gets to see them as human beings, not as statistics on an FBI file."

In a way, Vinnie and his co-stars are often on equal footing, which is rather unusual for network television.

"I knew as a writer that it would create a situation where [he] would be a counterpuncher, as opposed to carrying the action in a story," executive producer and co-creator Stephen J. Cannell told *Rolling Stone*. "My idea was that we would reinvent the show every half year."

Cannell had approached ABC with the series premise, but was rejected, and then went to CBS, who accepted the idea. He set upon

Ken Wahl portrays Federal Agent Vincent Terranova in WISEGUY

the task of writing the pilot, but found that he was saddled with end of the season "burn out," and needed a co-writer. So he approached Frank Lupo, part of the creative team behind such series as *Hunter* and *Hardball*.

"Stephen and I had worked together for years," explains Lupo. "We created *The A-Team*, *Riptide* and *Hunter* together. After I did *Hunter*, Stephen went off and did a couple of things on his own, and I did my thing, even though I was working for his company. We were both great fans of police dramas, mysteries that type of thing, and he came to me one day with an idea about doing a show about an undercover cop. But he wanted to do one from the point of view from inside the mob. I believe that Stephen originally had an offshoot of this idea, where it would be a show about mobsters, which is something he'd always wanted to do. But there had been a number of shows that had tried that. The problem was always the morality of the hero. He wasn't sure if a show like that could be done on a week to week basis. Sure, you could go in on something like *The Godfather* and could buy it for three hours, and then walk out, but he wasn't quite sure if every week we could maintain the morality of a hero was was totally on the wrong side.

"Anyway," he adds, "Stephen originally came to me with the idea of a cop who infiltrates the mob. I was buried in scripts and told him so, and he said that he had thought it was something we could have fun doing together, but he left. I remember driving home that night, thinking about it and I started writing stuff in my head. Two days later I walked in his office and said, 'Do you still want to do that **Wiseguy** idea?' We realized that it was well into the development part of the season, but we went in, pitched it and they said okay. I think we pitched it in early December and had to have the script done by Christmas. It was very fast, and we slammed it out very quickly, each of us writing half the pilot. We put the two halves together, and I think I was the first one to read it, and I found that we had somehow missed the Vinnie/Sonny relationship because we wrote it so quickly. Stephen came into my office and said, 'Well, how did we do?' And I just gave him the script to read, and he recognized the same problem with it I had."

Cannell agreed. "The story was told okay," he said, "but there was no relationship with anyone in the pilot script. There was a romantic skirmish with [Steelgrave's niece], and we considered trying to embellish on that. Then I said, 'Why don't we write Sonny Steelgrave as the relationship?' Frank looked at me and said, 'Butch and Sundance...'"

Revisions were made.

Lupo adds, "What we came up with was the idea of an undercover cop. We wanted to come up with a character that he could truly admire on the other side of the fence. As the whole Sonny Steelgrave story started, it was almost like a mini-series, rather than a pilot for a TV show. We knew that in the pilot he would meet Steelgrave, and that he would displace one of Sonny's lieutenants. We also knew he would move up to be his right hand man, and at that point we talked about the idea of doing a number of heavies each year in five or six episode arcs, so we had come up with that concept. We did know that we were going to build up the relationship between Vinnie and Sonny, so that by the time we hit the end, it wasn't going to just be an hour episode where someone pretends to be on someone's side, and at the end of the hour when he's busted, there's a tear in the eye of the cop,

but he's saying, 'We got you, asshole.' Needless to say, this kind of thing raised a few eyebrows at CBS, and they said to us, 'Couldn't Vinnie really be faking Sonny Steelgrave out? He doesn't have to truly admire him.' We said, 'You don't understand where we're coming from,' and their response was, 'It's going to be real clear that Vinnie's not going over, right?' We said, 'We're not sure. We will redeem him, but it has got to be enticing.' So it was that kind of reaction, but there wasn't a tremendous amount of resistance. All we really wanted was a relationship between Sonny and Vinnie and if we could get Vinnie through some of the dirt, he'd be able to see what made up the individual people.

"When we were putting the pilot together," Lupo continues, "we couldn't figure out where to start. We had one draft which started in Quantico when Vinnie first entered the Academy, and we have one where he's in the middle of the scam that he's in prison for at the beginning of the pilot. I would say the first half hour of the show would have been the one that got him locked up, and that was the kind of material we were testing, but in a pilot you have to give the network an idea of what the show will be like. Had we handed in these stories, it would say, 'Okay, this tells us that the series is coming, but not what the series would be.' By the time we were getting closer, working on the second story I mentioned, we felt it wasn't as far developed as the two hours that would eventually air. Then we said, 'You know, we've got to keep going; we should either write a three hour pilot or short-cut the front end.' We short-cut the front end, with the intent of always being able to do a flashback one day; a flashback which reveals how he went to Quantico and then to prison."

Second season Executive Story Editor John Schulian believes that the character relationships coupled with the Steelgrave arc originally attracted public attention to the series. "It proved that [Executive Producer] David Burke was right in what he wanted to do with the show," he says. "He's really the guy who has shaped this. He did not want to make it a constant series of car chases and gun fights. He subscribes to Steven Bochco's theory of emotional violence being infinitely more powerful than overt, physical violence. When Sonny looks at Vinnie after he's found out that he's a cop and says, 'I loved you, man,' and then electrocutes himself, it's a perfect example of this. That really is what this show is about."

"I just love characters," Burke concurs, "and I thought the relationship between Vinnie and Sonny was one he would like to maintain as a friendship, but can't because he knows the true stripes of the man. That was enticing. I'm not a big fan of gunplay, and **Wiseguy** presents the opportunity to actually spend time with characters and develop them fully. I think one of our greatest strengths is that we are able to give actors material they can really enjoy and sink their teeth into. That, for me, is the essential strength of what we do, and we've been real fortunate with performers; people who aren't afraid to play big moments and to play dialogue that is not traditional television."

Breaking with tradition has become the norm with **Wiseguy**.

THE MAKING OF A WISEGUY

Ken Wahl as Vinnie
Terranova in a typically
pensive mood

KEN WAHL

"When I would watch films and television," Ken Wahl once explained, "I just went from the standpoint that I think I might be able to do this. I didn't go out there cocky. I went out there wanting to be equal with the rest of the business. I had made up my mind before [I went to Hollywood] that I wasn't going to be a slave to the business. I think it really has a tendency to remove people's dignity, trying too hard. I didn't come in with a resume that was lies. I said I had never done anything before, but I recognized that it's a business thing. I said, 'I think I can do the job for you. If you want to give me a shot, let's do it.' And we did it."

What Wahl did was get a lead role in director Philip Kaufman's *The Wanderers*, which in turn led to roles in such films as Bette Midler's *Jinxed*, the Vietnam drama *Purple Hearts* and Paul Newman's *Fort Apache: The Bronx*. It is, however, for his three seasons on CBS' **Wiseguy** as OCB undercover operative Vincent Terranova that he is best known.

"When this show was offered to me, I wasn't really looking to do a television series because it's a very grinding work schedule," Wahl explained. "I read the pilot and and it was very good, and I wanted it and they wanted me and we made a deal and here we are."

He points out that there were some risks in accepting a series based on its pilot. "When you're doing a pilot, you have no idea even if the pilot's gonna be sold, and if it is, what the scripts are going to be. You're taking a big chance when you do a television series."

The chance has obviously paid off, as critics have often cited the show's unique aspects, commending his abilities at the same time. He was nominated for a 1988 Emmy Award for best dramatic actor.

Most intriguing to Wahl from the outset was the ambiguity of the storylines, where definitions of good and evil weren't as clear cut as on traditional television crime dramas.

"It wasn't just Gene Autry riding into town with his white hat on," Wahl's noted. "It's a lot more fun, because you can get away with just about anything. You can come in here and start chewing up the furniture, and it's OK, because you're supposed to be nuts. I must say that's one of my favorite things about this character. He's acting as well. Although when you're an actor acting a part, you're not living in constant fear—well, I guess some actors do—but with the character acting, there's a lot of underlying fear because you have to make sure you say the right thing all the time.

"The acting challenge," he told the press, "is that you have to give to the other characters in relationship to the storyline, enough to believe Vinnie playing that part. But on the other hand, Vinnie can't give too much away—the underlying fear and all of that—because the bad guys will catch on. But you do have to give some of that to the audience, so they know what's really going on. All of that is the toughest thing."

Making things easier is a first rate production team, that the actor (who was made a supervising producer for the show's third season) has nothing but praises for, and from his words you detect that he's really happy where he is.

"Luckily we have a very good, tight team that works on **Wiseguy**," he's enthused. "There's Les Sheldon, David Burke, Steve Kronish and Al Ruggerio. We're a good team, and they not only allow my input, but encourage it. [Second] season we had a storyline that had Jerry Lewis in it, and it was my idea to cast him. I thought of him because he was magnificent in *The King of Comedy*.

"I care a lot about this show and I care a lot about the guys I work with," he added. "There may be times that I'm difficult, but I'm not difficult for the sake of being difficult. There's a reason for it. As we all can be difficult. And we'll butt heads about ideas, but we all really do respect each other. Sometimes you win the arguments and sometimes you lose, but it seems that, I would say, 90% of the time, the person that wins the argument is correct."

If Wahl has received criticism for anything, it's that he seems *too* low key about the series, only doing interviews when pressured by the network.

"I'm very pragmatic about my profession," Wahl once detailed, "and the job on **Wiseguy**. I [never wanted] the promotion of the show to be more important than the show itself. I don't want people to watch the show because of what they know about me personally. I want them to watch the show because they think it's a good show, and if they don't, we shouldn't be there."

JONATHAN BANKS

*Prior to his co-starring stint on **Wiseguy**, actor Jonathan Banks was primarily known as one of film and television's great villains. Besides numerous guest shots on episodic television, he co-starred in such blockbuster films as 48 Hours and Beverly Hills Cop. But it is undoubtedly as Frank McPike , Vinnie Terranova's field director on **Wiseguy** that he is best known. In fact, he was nominated for a 1988 Emmy Award for best supporting actor in a dramatic series.*

I'm proud of (**Wiseguy**), but at the same time even though I know the talent that surrounds it, I always find myself thinking, "Gee, if we only had a few more hours; if we only had seven more days; if the writers weren't constantly under pressure," and all that stuff, we could really knock you out of your socks. I'm more disappointed when it's not up to what my expectations are, and I'm always aware that we're doing hour TV in a very short period of time, but that's what it's about as far as TV is concerned. Overall I'm proud of it, because people work real hard, and it was real nice to get the Emmy nomination as a sign of recognition.

There's no question about it. Probably part of that is that I'm a poor enough actor that I don't try to keep a constant line on the character [laughs]. The writers started to write what they would see. They began to warm him up and the Vinnie/Frank relationship got better, and that really is nice because it culminates in us being able to do something like going on a camping trip [second season], which is probably my favorite show of all. We just had such a good time doing it.

I try to be pretty moral and get wildly confused doing it, so I'm a lot like Frank. But then again I love to be near water and I like to be in shorts and a T-shirt, so I don't feel a lot like him at all. I think he works hard, and that's something I try to do as well. I'd worked with Cannell quite often over a period of years, and I always felt that Stephen was pretty damn good to me. When this thing came up, essentially they said, "Would you be interested in one of the characters in the pilot?" Then they came back and said, "Would you be interested in doing this continuing character?" At the time, I'd been trying to do primarily TV movies and films, and all of a sudden I was confronted with a steady paycheck, and I went ahead and did it. I've never had that, having kind of just rolled along with my career, so that part of it is nice, although I'm ready to do another character at this point.

As much as Banks loves the character of McPike he is beginning to question his continued playing of the role. "We'll see what this season brings," he says. "As long as they give me something to play that's a dilemma for the character.

If it comes to the point that Frank is just spouting exposition, then as nice as the paycheck is, it's time to move on. It's early enough in the season that I want to wait and see what happens before I answer that question any further.

If it goes another year, I guess I'd do it. I want to be involved with it as long as it's fun. Right now, it's a good time for this show. Whatever happens to it this year, I think everyone is trying really hard to give a good hour of television. I think in the longrun, this show really will have helped me. It's what every actor says, but I'd like to eventually go back to doing films and being able to hold out for things that are very special.

I know that David Burke and the rest of the writers are very good to me, and I think they appreciate what I bring to it as an actor, so I have a lot of trust in them. They'll do as much as they can.

I'm just glad we're out of the music arc. That's just not my favorite stuff, investigating the music business. For Jonathan Bank's money, I just don't care. Investigating the government (as a more recent arc has done), though, is wildly intriguing to me. I grew up in DC, not that that means I'm wildly knowledgeable [laughs]. By the way, there's a school that does a report on the ten least publicized stories of the year, and there are things in there that will curdle the blood with what the president has been involved in, or toxic waste and those kinds of things. I bring that up, because I would think that with an investigation within the government, the problems you would have to overcome would be immense; the fences that would be put up all around you. My mom was a secretary at the Treasury Department and later became a college professor, but during the McCarthy witch hunt, she worked for a lawyer at the Treasury Department who tried to clear his name after being named a Communist. It took something like ten years for him to clear his name, but over that time cleared his name, the whole idea of what happened—that misuse of power on McCarthy's part—is just incredible.

I don't know where David and all those guys are going with the arc, but to be in Washington, the remarkable thing is to go in to the Jefferson Memorial or Lincoln Memorial and read those words. It's wonderful. There were just some very noble things done and said that we're still the recipients of. I love the idea that it's because of Jefferson that we have free education, and he was labelled a heretic because he wanted freedom of religion. Yeah, this is more important in my life and many other people's lives than Dead Dog Records.

The thing that I have always loved about **Wiseguy** is the ambiguity of it; the moral ambiguity of who's good, who's bad and what's going on. Now we're talking about going off to do a storyline pertaining to drugs. The people who live in Colombia now are saying about the drug lords, "Gee, maybe we should leave them alone, because things are a lot better here since these guys are around." That's what I'm getting from the press. You hear those reports and it's like, Holy Mother of God, what *is* going on?

My girlfriend is Spanish, and her whole thing about democracy and liberty and how important it is, is that she'll tell you that as far as being able to walk down the streets in Madrid, under Franco's regime it was a safer place to walk. For the majority of people, it was a more repressed, tranquil life, but there's a trade-off for liberty. I hope the scripts for the arc really deal with some of that.

If you get somebody to think for just one second, it's a good thing. It sounds pompous when you say that, but if you take it to another place and say, "Well, there are a lot of kids out there from 16 to 18, their minds are wide open and if you stir them to a certain extent by watching something that's entertaining, great. Good for you." You can do it in

all kinds of different ways. I've never been a fan of *Little House on the Prairie* or *Highway to Heaven*, but at the same time, when I look back on it, you think about some of the messages that Michael Landon put through to a really young audience, and that ain't so bad. Good for him.

Out here we just had a girl who was shot in Westwood, a real nice place, when she got caught in the gunfire of a gang fight. All of these witnesses have been threatened, and they're middle class people who just happened to be in the same place. Some were not so middle class, some were poor people and some were richer, and what happened was that a lot of these witnesses went ahead and testified *anyway*. The dead girl's brother came out of the courtroom after the first witness—a kid from the valley—testified, and thanked him for having the courage to take the stand, to which the kid replied, "Hey, man, I had to do what was right." I just love it. As tripe as this sounds, there are some everyday heroes out there, and thank God, because there's a lot of crap out there too. What's going on out there ain't the best. I'll be 43 this year, and it's not a matter of talking to shoot off my mouth anymore. I've really got to live what I believe, because this whole thing is going to be over real quick. The first 43 years went by at a pace, to say the least, and I really feel it's important to live some of the things I have opinions about as far as voting, becoming involved, fighting for what I believe in, try-

ing to make it a better world, trying to go down there and work with people and kids who are less fortunate. Whatever it may be. Just talking about it—about anything—doesn't make any difference.

I have a feeling—and this has probably been triggered by the fact we're doing this Washington, DC arc—that if we all went back to the idea of town meetings and being involved with what goes on directly around us, with a greater knowledge of our own government, that there's a certain amount of not only excitement, but fun involved. Out here in Hollywood you become very isolated and there's not a real sense of community hardly anywhere. If more people were involved with their own communities, they'd end some of their own loneliness. They'd be putting their own minds to work, and they'd be making a difference.

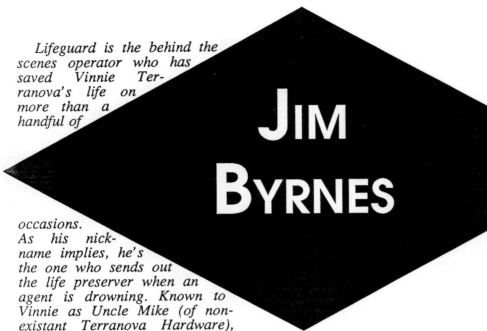

JIM BYRNES

Lifeguard is the behind the scenes operator who has saved Vinnie Terranova's life on more than a handful of occasions.

As his nickname implies, he's the one who sends out the life preserver when an agent is drowning. Known to Vinnie as Uncle Mike (of non-existant Terranova Hardware), Lifeguard is a paraplegic, a condition which is of no consequence to his functioning as an operative of the OCB.

Season one essentially kept Lifeguard in his communication center, but the following two years have seen the show's writers bring him out of those confines to explore the underlying aspects of the character. They've defined the bond of friendship between Vinnie, Frank and Lifeguard.

To actor Jim Byrnes, this is all very gratifying. A paraplegic in real life, he has struggled, in his own words, for 20 years to develop a career in music and acting. Now, it seems as though he has scored on both counts, as Wiseguy is in its third year, and his blues band "Jim Byrnes" is starting to garner attention.

We have a script coming up where they come to my actual apartment, and it's filled with books. I'm there cooking, which is kind of interesting, because we had not talked about it at all, but I love to cook and I'm the cook of my own house. It's funny how the thing goes. I guess as you get to know the writers, they sense certain things about you, which is what makes them good. You don't want to play yourself, but it's nice to add some sort of hook so you can make the guy that much more

real. I'd say we meet about halfway.

(One example of this serendipity was in the background the writers created as explanation of how Lifeguard became paraplegic.) A situation where they (the writers) didn't know what had happened to me and yet it was extremely similar. We did have one discussion where they were talking about making this guy a war hero, and I wanted to make it as real as we could.

I became involved with the show while I'd been living here in Vancouver for about ten years, and traveled with my band up and down the West Coast. At the same time, I wanted to be an actor and had studied to be one, but because of my accident I hadn't been able to get any parts and kind of had to put it on the back burner and really concentrate on the music. But there was so much stuff going on in Vancouver in terms of film and television that I really was anxious to get involved and give it a shot. I spoke to some people, and one night I came back from a trip and had a message on my machine that there was a show where there might be a part. Y'know, the audition may be only for a couple of lines, but it might have turned into something. I didn't really care. I just thought it was a great opportunity, because they're few and

far between once people hear about my condition, which is pretty frustrating. I'd go to an audition and they'd say, "Oh, we really can't use you." I just showed up, read for the part of Lifeguard and had a real good rapport with them. Les Sheldon Jr., our executive producer, and Rod Holcomb, who directed the pilot, were great and everything went well, and I thought, "Well, that was positive." I went home and I got a phone call back from them saying that they felt the same way, so they brought me down again in front of a video camera. I know they had a lot of people read for the part, but out of all of them I got picked. There's a certain amount of fate involved, I guess, and it's one of those things where you get a lucky break. I've worked hard for the last 20 years trying to get a lucky break.

The original script said the guy (Lifeguard) comes in long haired, paraplegic and in a wheelchair. That helped, because I came in while I was walking with my prosthetics. When I got the part, I myself thought, "Gee, if I'm going to be zipping around this loft in a wheelchair, I would not have my prosthesis on; it would get in the way. On the road they're great, but not while I'm in a chair. I was about to tell them that idea, when I got a phone call saying, "We were wondering if you would mind...."

When they wrote this part, it was never written with anyone feeling sorry for this guy, because there's nothing to feel sorry for. At the same time, we were trying to fight from making him super human. We wanted to make him a real person with his own problems, one of which is that he's limited physically, but his biggest problem in his emotional alienation from his loved ones, and that's why we've had lots of positive response from groups around the country. We just tell it like it is. We don't make an issue out of it. It's black and white. I live with this every day and I don't talk about it, I just do what I've got to do. That's one thing I've got to say about Stephen Cannell. He's done that on some of his other shows, like *Hunter* used real deaf actors. It's ridiculous when there are talented people out there who can be used, to use somebody else. It's a great opportunity for me and a lot of other actors. It's educational to people who don't know about the problem, who have the problem themselves and say, "Look at this guy, he's like me." And it's a good, positive image to be presenting.

These guys are all over the emotional plane, and they've all got problems.

(The series press kit carries a quote by Byrnes that reads, "Lifeguard is good because he's good, not because he's crippled.")

Actually I got that from Ray Charles, when he said, "I'm not good because I'm blind, I'm good because I'm good," which makes its own point, that you do what you've got to do.

(Wahl, Banks and me) are not a rat pack or anything, but we do share one another's confidence and respect, and that's one thing that I think is very important and helps in terms of the relationship we have on the show. We do go out now and then, or I'll have them over for a family dinner. We're buddies, and when we've got a problem, we'll say it.

I still wake up every day and am amazed. I'm still pinching myself that it's finally happening for me. Sometimes, and I don't know why I feel this way, but I look over my shoulder and say, "Oh, oh. Something bad's going to happen. Everything's going too good." I try not to do it too much because you bring it upon yourself if you do. But it feels good and I'd like to get another year out of the show. We're not looking to go on for too long or else you start imitating yourself. We're just taking it as long as it goes along honestly. I'm very happy with my position. It's opened a lot of doors for me both with acting and music. I've gotten some scripts and I may be

able to look at them when I have some time off. The music is really starting to move now. It's been extremely positive and I've learned a lot working with Kenny and John, Ray, Kevin Spacey, Jerry Lewis and all the people who have been on the show. I like to go down to the set, even when I'm not working, to see these people at work. One of the things I love about music and acting is that you can never be good enough; there's always something new to learn. It's a constant learning process, of change and evolution. At this time, with the things going on with the show, the music and my baby, I'm the luckiest guy in the world.

'd like to have a record and gain more recognition than I have. I would really like to keep on doing what I'm doing. Obviously **Wiseguy** can't go on forever. I'd love to get some feature work. My agent and I are working on getting something where we make absolutely no mention of the fact that I walk with a cane. That's really a goal of mine, not that I have any problem talking about it, but people don't talk about guys who wear glasses. That's something I hope happens. I want to keep acting and performing with my band until I fall over. As I said, it's a constant learning process for me.

SEASON ONE
STEELGRAVE

"Wiseguy": The Pilot

Original Airdate: 9/16/87
Written by Stephen J. Cannell and Frank Lupo
Directed by Rod Holcomb
Starring: Ken Wahl, Jonathan Banks, Jim Byrnes

Guest Starring: Ray Sharkey, Gianni Russo, Robert Miranda, Jessica Steen, Gerald Anthony, John Wesley, John M. Jackson, Jack Ging, Mark Rolston, Leon Pownall and Adriana Baron, Alar Aedma, William Taylor, Alex Diakun, David Burner, Tom Heaton, Peter Chapek, Adam Yawrenkno, Alex Bruhanski, Gary Chalk, Ralph Cole, Frank C. Turner, Sydney Filkow, Dwight Koss and Coleen Winton.

Vinnie and Sonny develop a brotherly relationship, despite Terranova's assignment to bring Steelgrave's organization down

The pilot for **Wiseguy** begins with Vincent Terranova being released from a federal penitentiary after serving 18 months. He is brought to OCB headquarters by his new field supervisor, Frank McPike, where he meets up with OCB Director Daryl Elias, who wants to put him right into his assignment as an undercover officer. Vinnie says that he can't just yet, because he has a mother with a heart condition who's suffering over the fact that her son is a hood. He wants to tell her that he's really a cop, which Elias tells him he absolutely can't do. Terranova is ready to quit.

In the meantime, Vinnie's original training officer, due for imminent retirement, goes out to meet an informer who will provide him with enough information to take down New Jersey mobsters Dave and Sonny Steelgrave. However he's betrayed, and it's Dave Steelgrave who steps out of the shadows, and shoots him at point blank range.

Vinnie goes to the hospital and shares the man's last moments of life, swearing that he'll bring down the Steelgrave organization. Later, he goes to see his brother, Father Pete Terranova, to discuss what's going on. Pete, we quickly learn, is aware of Vinnie's true identity, and when Vinnie says he wants to see their mother, Pete warns him off of the idea, stating that it would upset her too much. The only way they should be brought together is if Vinnie tells her that he's a cop, which he's not quite ready to do.

Going back to OCB headquarters, Vinnie makes it clear that he's ready to resign, but then he's given the Steelgrave assignment. From there, he gets a job as a waiter in a restaurant that the Steelgraves frequent, and manages to pick a fight with Sonny, who's right hand, Tony Greco, wants to take care of Vinnie. Sonny won't hear of it, telling Vinnie to meet him at his pier in warehouse three, where they'll settle the whole thing.

Later, the two men—both of whom have a background in golden gloves boxing—are fighting each other, and it looks as though Vinnie will beat Sonny, until he uncurls his fists, and lowers his guard. Sonny takes advantage of this, pummels him and knocks him to the ground. "You had me," he whispers, crouching down. He thinks for a moment, and tells Vinnie to meet him at his casino. The Steelgraves leave, while Greco stands around a moment longer, to deliver a savage kick to Vinnie's gut.

Vinnie arrives at the casino. Meeting with Sonny, and being formally introduced to Dave [and there is a wonderful shot of Vinnie and Dave shaking hands, with Sonny sitting in the middle—symbolic, no doubt, of the torn feelings he will have later in this arc], Vinnie is told that Sonny is surprised he showed up at the warehouse. Vinnie points out that if he doesn't take himself seriously, how can he expect others to. Sonny is impressed. He brings Vinnie to a loft in the casino, tells him he can stay there and offers him a job as a driver. Vinnie agrees, and is told to get a new suit and the car cleaned. Sonny does, however, add one ominous note: mess up, and he might get dropped in a hole on the turnpike.

Sonny and Vinnie go to one of the mobster's casinos to pick up $15,000 from Gravedigger Jones, who claims that five people hit "the number" in a row, thus cleaning out much of the evening's proceeds. Sonny demands the money and makes threats in his own subtle way. Gravedigger gives him the money, and once the duo have left, tells his men to follow Sonny's car, waste both of them and bring his money back. It's only a moment or two before Sonny and Vinnie realize they're being followed. Vinnie pulls into a gas station, then rams one of the cars. He and Sonny get out of the car armed with baseball bats, and overpower the men, with Vinnie stealing their wallets and jewelry. This, too, impresses Sonny.

Next, they proceed to the pier, which features a large sign that reads "Greco's Marine," where Tony gets a call saying that someone named Winfield has pulled in. Sonny wants him to find out what Winfield has been doing, because things haven't been going right on the dock, and he wants Tony to bring Vinnie with him. Moments later, Winfield is pulled into the car, shouting, "What are you doing, Tony? I paid you!" Vinnie's suspicion is aroused.

They arrive at an amusement park and a small booth near a roller coaster. Tony drags Winfield inside, and tells Vinnie to remain outside. As soon as the door is closed, Vinnie makes his way to the roof, sees the lights within the booth dimming and hears Winfield screaming, which indicates some form of electrocution. He moves back to the ground just as Tony steps outside, and is told to leave Winfield alone. Tony locks the door, and says he'll be back with Dave Steelgrave. Once Tony is gone, Vinnie taps on the door, asking if Winfield is okay. There's no response.

Dave and Tony arrive, open the door and find that Winfield is dead. Tony accuses Vinnie, which infuriates him, and Dave is livid, telling them that they can't get answers from a dead guy. He wants Winfield buried "deep." Tony and Vinnie put Winfield's body in the trunk, and they take off, only to be stopped moments later by a pair of cops who are continually harassing Steelgrave's people. As they get out of their car and approach the limo, Tony pulls a gun and is intent on blowing them away. Vinnie, seeing himself with no alternative, puts the car in reverse, smashes their squad car and takes off.

Tony and Vinnie arrive at the pier, where Dave and Sonny have found crates of weapons. They're told that

Winfield had signed for them, but the cargo ship is empty. Sonny announces that they're going to sell the weapons back to their owner. Turning his attention to Vinnie, he tells him to get back to the casino until the heat dies down. Enroute, though, Vinnie is arrested (an arrest orchestrated by the OCB), and he asks Frank to gather all information available on Winfield.

Vinnie is bailed out by Sonny, and returns to the casino. Eventually Lifeguard informs him of the room number of the hotel Winfield checked into. He goes there and encounters a mysterious Latino beauty, learning that the weapons belongs to a Mr. Sykes. If they want the merchandise back, they should call him at a number he leaves. If they take too long, he'll dump the crates.

Vinnie goes to a gym, where Sonny is watching his boxers work out. He's delighted to learn that Vinnie has obtained the information on Sykes. Tony is immediately suspicious, but Vinnie explains he checked the phone book and called every hotel and motel in the area until he found the right one. This is good enough for Sonny, but not for Greco.

That afternoon, Vinnie, Dave, Sonny, Tony and a few others have a meeting with Sykes and his woman. Sykes explains that he paid Winfield $100,000 to use the pier, and wants to know why he should pay for items he already owns. Tony, who runs the pier, says Winfield never said anything about it. Then, Vinnie hears something in the next room and goes to check on it. There he finds Sykes' men with machine guns aimed at the wall. They begin firing, and Vinnie eliminates them. He proceeds back to the other room, where he finds Sykes gone, Dave dead, Tony wounded and Sonny barely alive.

That night at the pier, the Latino kills two men, and Sykes has the crates put back on his boat. Vinnie finds out, calls Lifeguard and tells him to put $100,000 in Greco's account, and to make sure it's known that the cash was deposited by "a good looking Latino woman."

Going to the hospital, Vinnie sees Sonny, who wants to know what happened. Where was Vinnie when everything went down? He also points out that things started going lousy as soon as he showed up. Tony suggests that Vinnie set them up, but he counters that things were in motion long before he arrived on the scene, and he provides an alternate possibility: maybe Tony was given the $100,000 by Winfield. Refusing to dismiss any possibility, Sonny tells one of his people to check it out. Greco is shocked. "Sonny, I've been with you for 20 years...."

Apparently angry and hurt, Greco leaves. Vinnie tells Sonny that Sykes didn't get away with anything. He put rocks in the crates, which is all they brought out to sea. Sonny doesn't know what to make of this, noting that Vinnie moves fast....maybe too fast. The ship is called, and Sonny tells Sykes that he'll get his weapons if he pays the price. Sykes agrees. Then, Sonny is told that Greco's account had $100,000 deposited in it by a Spanish woman.

Moments later, Vinnie goes to an outside pay phone and calls Lifeguard. Greco catches him, Vinnie leaves the phone dangling (which allows everything said to be recorded, and the line to be traced) and Greco says that everything he thought was right, but it doesn't matter, because he's going to kill him. Vinnie tells Greco that Sonny is looking for him, because they found $100,000 in his account.

"You think I'm stupid enough to deposit the money?" he asks.

"I deposited it for you."

Cops arrive, and Vinnie takes advantage of the distraction to deck Greco. He's taken into custody by Frank, who promises that Greco will never get out of prison while Vinnie is under cover.

Vinnie then arrives at the pier, where the final battle is played out. There are helicopters, machine guns, rocket launchers and the like. But after a wide variety of explosions, Vinnie and Sonny's people prove victorious. The cops arrive and Vinnie is arrested again.

At Dave's funeral, Sonny expresses doubts about Vinnie, but Vinnie tries to defend himself by saying that Greco's disappearance must prove something. Their conversation is interrupted by a Federal officer, Hawthorne, who continues his harassment of Sonny, refers to Dave as a greaseball and mentions that Greco has been talking to them. Sonny wants to do him, and tells Vinnie that if he "wastes this Fed, I'll trust you forever."

That night, Vinnie rings a doorbell, Hawthorne opens the door, and Vinnie shoots him point blank, slamming the body backwards, apparently dead. Vinnie and Sonny leave, and no sooner have they gone than Frank comes down the stairs. Hawthorne gets to his feet, and the two of them talk about the relocation program.

Outside, Sonny looks at Vinnie with a newfound respect. "You're through being a driver. You're getting Greco's action. Hey, kid, you're moving up."

Although the last fifteen minutes or so of the pilot seemed a bit more like a James Bond adventure than the series that would eventually unfold, **Wiseguy** was off to a hell of a start. Most notably, the groundwork was laid down for interesting relationships between Vinnie and McPike, and, particularly, Vinnie and Sonny. It is undeniable that there is chemistry between Ken Wahl and Ray Sharkey, and it's reassuring to know that this was only the beginning. The best was yet to come.

CBS liked the pilot enough to green light a weekly series. Cannell brought together his creative staff for the show, which included supervising producers (now executive producers) David J. Burke and Stephen Kronish, and story editor Eric Blakeney. Both Burke and Blakeney had previously worked together on Michael Mann's *Crime Story*, and looked at **Wiseguy** as an opportunity to continue challenging the boundaries of the medium.

"I didn't love the pilot," Blakeney admits, "but I thought there was tremendous potential there. I enjoyed the first half, although it was a little fantastic. The whole idea that you could beat the shit out of a Mafia chief and have him bring you into the fold was a bit ludicrous to me, but there was something in the relationship that really turned me on. The second half of the pilot, with the terrorist, machine guns and helicopters was just standard TV violence and didn't do anything for me. As I said, there was potential there, and David and I said, 'Let's just get in there and take this baby over and bring out the good stuff.'"

David Burke notes, "I realized that I'd always wanted to write for Ray and I thought Ken was magnetic. Together they were great. Also, there were things in the pilot that bothered me about the character, such as Vinnie keeping his life secret from his mother. That, for me, was fodder for good satisfying drama. I just love characters, and am not a big fan of gunplay, though I suppose if you looked at the shows I've worked on, you wouldn't know that. I like relationships and things that are political. This show had all the opportunities to write the things I wanted to write. When we got into it, the show guided us as much as we guided the show in terms of the relationships that developed."

Blakeney, who currently serves as Executive Producer of Ray Sharkey's new private eye series to air on ABC in fall 1990, points out that there was tremendous energy involved at the outset, as the staff felt they were producing something that was new and different.

"In Ray Sharkey," he says, "we had the most appealing villain that had ever been on television, because of his tremendously human qualities. For me, the biggest turn on about doing **Wiseguy** was that I would get an opportunity to work with a villain who wasn't a cut out; who wasn't a pure evildoer. And in Kenny Wahl's character, there was an opportunity to work with a guy who had much more complex psychological and emotional problems, who wasn't just coming on television every week saying, 'Beware, Evildoers.' I felt that the series eventually lost that, but in the beginning it was incredible.

"I should point out that during the Sonny Steelgrave arc, I was the biggest pain in the ass in terms of my insistence on what we did with this relationship," Blakeney continues with a laugh. "In many ways, they gave me tremendous leeway for my position, and I'm grateful for that. But I was really turned on by the whole concept of the good things that bad people do and the bad things that good people do. I think that's where you find drama. For me, there's no drama in a guy who does the right thing all the time. There's no conflict. He'll always do the right thing, and it's really just a question of will he single-handedly be able to defeat 70,000 screaming maniacs with uzis. Well, of course he can. We've got to put him on the air next week. There's never truly any jeopardy on prime time television. Your hero will always win. In this show there were many more complexities.

"As far as I was concerned, Kenny (Ken Wahl/Vinnie) was written as a betrayer. Basically he was a morally good and righteous guy who became very confused by the realities of the world in that it's very hard to always do the right thing. He was a de facto good guy in that he went in there to arrest the bad guy, but he was betraying a friend. And Sonny Steelgrave was completely open and honest and gave himself over to this relationship, and he was the bad guy. In the relationship between the two of them, Sharkey was pure and Kenny was the deceiver, and that for me was the series. That was the turn on. I mean, Sonny was a fool to his emotions, and that's what was so wonderful about it. Many times he had Vinnie caught, and our attempts at saving Vinnie were pretty lame. In other words, he was coming up with some hokey excuse to get out of it. What really was happening here was a guy who loved this other guy so much. He lost his brother, he embraced a surrogate brother and was blind to Brutus. He'd fallen in love with his betrayer."

Les Sheldon adds, "What we constantly try to do is explore the characters. We all pull on the same rope, and we're all trying to explore the same type of human beings. What we try to do is bring something interesting to that human being through the course of an arc, therefore we're able to attract incredible artists. And as artists they want to portray human beings. We give them the opportunity to fully explore who they're playing, as opposed to just 48 minutes of television."

From the outset, the difference between **Wiseguy** and every other crime show was obvious. Dramatic elements that had been laid down in the pilot were fleshed out over the subsequent episodes that made up the first arc, beginning with "New Blood."

"New Blood"

Original Air Date: 9/24/87

Written by David J. Burke

Directed by Lyndon Chubbock

Guest Starring: Ray Sharkey, Joe Dallesandro, Eric Christmas, Dennis Lipscomb, Vic Polizos, Joe Shea, Kevin McNulty, Frank Ferrucci, Morris Panych, Fred Pleasure, Craig Brunanski, Jano Frandsen, Lynn P. Johnson and Sam Kouth

With the death of his brother Dave, Sonny finds himself in an extremely vulnerable position. Prosecutor Anthony Sererra announces his plan to bring down Steelgrave Industries, which has the double effect of jeopardizing Vinnie's undercover assignment, while giving other *families* cause to see this as an opportunity to take over Sonny's interests in Atlantic City.

Paul "Pat the Cat" Patrice has Sonny meet with him in a bowling alley, where he says that he wants to send a team of men into Sonny's organization to help "manage" things. Sonny is against the idea, handing his gun to Patrice and saying that he wants to be shot between the eyes. "Let me die like a man," says Sonny. "I won't let you castrate me."

Patrice, who has a major investment in Steelgrave Industries, considers this for a moment, then asks that Sonny accept an accountant, a man named Syd Royce, to

Ray Sharkey as mob kingpin Sonny Steelgrave

help organize things. Reluctantly, Sonny agrees. Then he has to deal with Mack "No Money" Mahoney who feels that he has to put someone in as well. "You let New York put a man in," he says. "Philadelphia's got interests too." Again, he has no choice, so he accepts Harry the Hunch, considered to be the mob's equivalent of a historian.

The rest of the episode unfolds with Patrice and Syd discreetly framing Sonny with an assassination attempt on Sererra. Finding them on the scene of said attempt, the police arrest Sonny and Vinnie. Frank finds himself in the unenviable position of having to use Federal clout to free the man they're trying to take down, but, as Vinnie points out, it's necessary if they're going to destroy the entire organization. A curve ball comes when Sonny cuts a deal, and all Vinnie has to do is take a lie-detector test. This goes well, until he's asked whether or not he works for Sonny Steelgrave and he replies in the affirmative, though the machine disagrees.

Later, back in his office, Sonny wants to know what secret Vinnie is hiding. Vinnie counters that he was a nervous wreck through the whole test, and that he chewed up the inside of his mouth trying to trick the machine. He feels that Sonny doesn't tell him everything, so he's not fully aware of what's going on, thus it's impossible for him to answer many of the questions honestly. Sonny accepts this, though tentatively at first.

Through Harry the Hunch's lecture about the way things used to be, Vinnie comes to the conclusion that a pizzeria located across the street from Sererra's office is actually mob connected, and that one of the delivery people, Angelo, is actually an assassin. He and Sonny make it to Angelo's home and find the remnants of a home-made explosive as well as the radio-controlled detonator. They grab it and head to Sererra's office, where they find that they're too late. Angelo is on his way upstairs with his explosive, while the prosecutor is in the midst of a conversation with Frank McPike. Vinnie is sweating bullets, when Sonny, in fury, accidentally presses the control switch on the detonator, thus destroying Angelo, the elevator he was in and part of the building, while inadvertently saving the lives of Frank and Sererra.

"New Blood" is an effective follow-up to the **Wiseguy** pilot, settling into the tone and scale of the regular series without the pyrotechnics of its predecessor. Again we're able to see the bonding of Vinnie and Sonny, though at this point there is no confusion of loyalties on Vinnie's part. This was also the first of several examples of how Sonny sensed that everything wasn't quite right with Vinnie, but chose to ignore it, perhaps out of his need for someone to replace his brother in his heart.

A highlight of the episode is Sonny's description of how Patrice got the nickname "Pat the Cat," when in their youth a bunch of the current mob power brokers made a bet as to how far down their pants someone could put an alley cat. Patrice managed to get it all the way down, thus earning his moniker. Sonny is hysterical recounting this tale, delighting in the fact that Patrice couldn't straighten up for a week. Vinnie asks what happened to the cat, and Sonny grows much more solemn, explaining that the cat was torched and sent off running, until it was "toast." This is an undeniably chilling moment, and it's interesting to detect compassion from Sonny for an alley cat.

"For me," begins David Burke, "'New Blood' was a yardstick for me and my future involvement and creative influence with the show. For that reason, it was very, very important and it also introduced a whole bunch of characters that played out for the rest of that arc. It was Steelgrave's confrontation with Patrice, Mahoney's first appearance, as well as Harry the Hunch and Syd Royce. All of these people were important to introduce, because they helped to define Atlantic City as a territory. What that episode also did was define a battleground for the mob; a battleground that Steelgrave found himself in the center of after the death of his brother. That was real important and an opportunity for Stephen Kronish, myself and the rest of the writing staff to focus on real concrete confrontations problems that Vinnie found himself caught up in.

"What I'm thinking about in particular," he elaborates, "is almost all the first act, and certainly from the moment they go to the bowling alley and meet with Patrice to the point later on in the car between Sonny and Vinnie, where Steelgrave explains how Pat "the cat" Patrice got his nickname. I think the number of pages devoted almost solely to dialogue in this scene was something that hadn't happened much before, and that was real important for me. Two guys sitting in a car talking for four pages was an unusual circumstance, but it worked. My fondest recollection of that episode was that I could do that at all."

For director Lyndon Chubbock, things didn't go quite as wonderfully as he would have liked.

"'New Blood' was a living nightmare all the time," he explains. "You know how television works. You prep a show for seven days and you shoot for seven, so you have seven days to hire your cast, find your locations and do all the preproduction work. Well, a day into my prep the Director's Guild strike started, and they struck about half the companies in Hollywood, while the other half locked us out. They, in essence, fired me from **Wiseguy**, because I'm a member of the Director's Guild, and hired a Canadian director. But the strike only lasted one day, so they rehired me. But we ended up doing the first episode of the series with about three days prep. For the first episode, you should have had *twice* the normal time. In the middle, Ray got the flu and couldn't work for a couple of days. He tried to hang in there, and we ended up having to shoot straight through some nights. One day we had 75 set ups, and 25 on another, just to make up some of the time we lost. It was a very tough experience.

"From my point of view, the crux of the problem goes back to the point when I was not involved with the show during the strike," Chubbock says. "They hired actors that I would not have hired. I wanted to hire Bill Hickey as Harry the Hunch. Now Bill has a bad reputation as a drinker, and I don't know if it was that or the money, but while I was not on the show—and remember, I have casting authority as director—they hired this guy named Eric Christmas, and he did not deliver the kind of performance we wanted. That was the source of a problem between David Burke and I. It was like he was blaming me, but he's the guy who hired Eric.

"At any rate, that was the downside. Most of it circled around our short lack of prep and not being prepared to do this show to start off with. I think if we had more time, it would have been smoother, everyone would have been happier and everything would have gone better. But Ray Sharkey was fabulous to work with, Ken Wahl was great. I don't know how they are now, but in the first episode they were perfect. The whole cast was good.

"One thing you have to understand is that doing the first episode of any series is really like putting your head in the mouth of a lion, because you're going in without knowing what their expectations are and there are so many more opportunities to fail than there are to succeed. But I thought the script was great. I thought, 'This is some of the best television writing I've ever read.' It just had such a voice to it. Instead of just being very generic, it was very well written and I thought the idea was pure David Burke. I think he's tough to work with and has some very driven eccentricities, but he makes up for it with his talent as a writer. I think if you can pull that off, that's fine.

"The one thing I can really say about **Wiseguy** is that when I worked there," he concludes, "these people were really striving for quality and striving to make something good. So many people you work for in television are just striving to make *something*. Les Sheldon, David Burke and Stephen Kronish, really were men that were trying to make something a cut above television; something special. Maybe that's why I would forgive them for whatever they might do, because they are really there for long hours, with great dedication to a quality show. They're like film-makers. A lot of guys crank out a lot of TV shows, and if they don't work out, they go on to the next one. These guys are not that way at all. They're very dedicated and very intense about **Wiseguy**."

"The Loose Cannon"

Original Air Date 10/1/87

Written by Stephen J. Cannell

Directed by Larry Shaw

Guest Starring: Ray Sharkey, Joe Dallesandro, Gerald Anthony, Dennis Lipscomb, David Marciano, Yvette Heyden, Raymond Forchion, Blue Mankuma, Beverly Hendry and Venus Terzo

In "The Loose Cannon," Sonny is still trying to hold on to his criminal empire which is being slowly eaten away at by Patrice via Syd Royce. Compounding his troubles is the arrival of his nephew from Sicily, Lorenzo, who he hasn't seen in 16 years. It's obvious from the moment this guy arrives that something's not quite right with him—he's crazy! He picks fights with everyone, including Vinnie, and then tries to cut himself into Sonny's action, by single handedly launching an attack against a street gang that has been holding out on Steelgrave Industries. Sonny's attitude has been to let things blow over, Syd has stated that Patrice wants something done about them, or he'll send someone in to do it for him; and Lorenzo has brought everything to a head. The situation between Sonny and Lorenzo culminates in Sonny's kicking him out, telling him that the next time he leaves it'll be in a body bag. Lorenzo departs, intent on solidifying his own base of power.

Vinnie, meanwhile, is having his own share of problems in a relationship with one Gina Augustina, the widow of a cop who killed himself. She suspects that he's a cop as well, but can't prove it, and he, of course, can't let her know the truth, particularly not while he's in the midst of this undercover assignment. Ultimately he decides that he has to break up with her, although it's the last thing he really wants to do.

Unfortunately, Vinnie finds himself inextricably linked with both Lorenzo and Gina. First off, he discovers from McPike that this Lorenzo might very well be one of Sicily's most feared murderers, who killed the real Lorenzo right before he was supposed to set sail for America, and essentially took his identity. Since Vinnie can't tell Sonny about this, he's forced to deal with the situation on his own, and finds that he must act quicker when he learns that Lorenzo has gone to Gina's apartment. Arriving there, Vinnie finds the two of them, Lorenzo already having raped her and planning on doing it again. Through a verbal confrontation, Vinnie convinces Lorenzo to let her go, so that it'll be just between the two of them. Immediately after doing this, Lorenzo makes it clear that he knows Vinnie is a cop, because he read a letter Gina was writing in which she had come to this conclusion on her own. He offers a deal: let him go, and he won't tell Sonny the truth. Vinnie won't budge, which doesn't faze Lorenzo in the least. In fact, he says he's going to walk across the room, take the gun from Vinnie's hand, kill him, rape Gina again, kill her and place both their bodies on the front lawn like statues. Lorenzo makes a move for him, and Vinnie's response is to pull the trigger of his gun, blowing the man away in cold blood.

That final shot was really quite a jolt for the audience, and for those working on the show as well. It does, however, seem that actor David Marciano carried on to a great degree, detailing his plans in order to justify Vinnie's shooting him.

Director Larry Shaw explains, "At the time, I felt that David was going on kind of too long, but after seeing it several times, it seems right. Vinnie does have an option of going a different way. The guy does not have a gun, he's just pissed Vinnie off really bad. I think it was set up that way to make sure you don't lose sympathy for Vinnie."

David Burke notes that Vinnie's justification for this action was most definitely there. "It would have felt more justified had the move for Vinnie been as obvious as it was in the script. There, he really jumped at him, and he didn't do that in the actual execution of it."

"We had problems with the ending," adds Eric Blakeney. "As I recall, there were a lot of debates on how we should actually end it. We'd done several different endings, and I think one of the problems was in the way we were structuring the piece. We were a little worried about how we would handle the girl once she'd been tainted and raped. Structurally, we changed where Vinnie and she split up, so it wouldn't look like he dumped her because of what had happened. But we had to absolutely justify Vinnie's killing him, because it was a bold move to have your hero kill that way. Basically it's not a shoot out, and you can't have your hero shoot somebody in cold blood, so we had to turn the thread up as much as possible. I think it was an interesting moment in the series, even with us trying to please the forces that be. I don't know how it came off. To me, it was a moment that was justified, because he made it perfectly clear that he was going to kill Vinnie and that we was going to rape the girl again, so I think all Vinnie could do was pull the trigger. It did, however, have subtle ramifications, because you could debate whether a cop should have just wounded him and brought him in, or killed him. That was a bold step for television."

"There are times when Vinnie takes advantage of his position of being an agent," Wahl once commented. "He blew that guy away and got away with it. He got away with murder. [But] that's what I like about it so much. He's not always just a goody-two-shoes guy."

It's pointed out that such an action conveys to the audience that the people involved with the series were *not* kidding around.

"We weren't," Blakeney smiles. "We really wanted to pull out all of the cartoon cliches. We'd all done a lot of cop shows, and David and I had done *Crime Story* together. We both really became frustrated by the way the villains in that show became a bunch of rabid nincompoops, and we liked the challenge that **Wiseguy** presented. At the time, there was also a lot of energy and competition on the writing staff. It was interesting, because we were bringing out the best in each other, just the way that Lennon and McCartney did. It's so vain to compare it that way, but I can't think of another good comparison. If Lennon would do 'Strawberry Fields,' then McCartney would have to do 'Penny Lane.' I think we had that at the beginning, and we were on to a good thing."

"On a lighter note," Burke interjects, "my biggest recollection was David Marciano, who turned in a performance that actually had Ray Sharkey on his toes. Ray was like, 'Whoa, this kid's got me hopping here. He's making moves I don't think I'd make,' so for that reason it was fun."

Blakeney clarifies. "Ray is a pro," he says. "Ray likes the competition. A lot of guys, if they're faced with a powerful actor, get pissed and want the guy the hell out of there. The first thing they do is say the script is bad and certain scenes are no good, and those are generally the scenes where the other guy is upstaging them. That's a standard Hollywood problem with actors. Ray is not like that at all. His attitude is, 'Give him his best shot. I want to get in there with him.'

"What was also funny," he points out, "is that the script was too long. Being a political innocent, I edited some of Cannell's dialogue and the whole company freaked. Everybody liked me and was really great with me at that point, but they were saying, 'My God, you can't edit Cannell's dialogue.' I had a phone call from

Cannell coming in and everyone was pacing. Then he calls and says, 'Nice job, Eric.' It was really exciting, and everyone's reaction was pretty funny."

"The Birthday Surprise"

Original Air Date 10/8/87
Written by Eric Blakeney
Directed by Robert Iscove

Guest Starring: Ray Sharkey, Eric Christmas, Gerald Anthony, Dennis Lipscomb, Aharon Ipale, Nestor Serrano, Sal Lopez, Richard Lion and Eddie Ross Pagliaro

Sonny and Vinnie are attending amateur fights at Steelgrave's Diamond Casino, where Vinnie's cousin, Danny Tessio, is boxing. While there, Sonny is approached by Kiki Vanno who tells him two things: one, he can fix the amateurs and "bigger things" anytime that Sonny wants him to, and that a gentleman by the name of Minos Zaratzo would like to have some of his time. Kiki doesn't even flinch when Sonny responds that private consultations are a million dollars a session. Eventually Zaratzo tells Sonny that he would like to use Steelgrave controlled lines of passage to transport merchandise. At first Sonny is reluctant, but the price eventually goes to his liking, although Zaratzo isn't too pleased with the amount he has to pay.

While this is going on, tragedy strikes Vinnie's life on his birthday when he learns that Danny has been found dead, the victim of a drug overdose. Absolutely positive that his cousin never used drugs, he begins a personal vendetta to find his killer. Feeling the pain that this surrogate brother is going through, particularly when considering the pain he himself felt when his brother Dave was killed, Sonny swears that they'll find Danny's killer, which is what Vinnie wants more than anything. In fact, later on he even goes to the point of flashing his OCB badge to the coroner to get more details, a fact which infuriates Frank. So incensed is he at this, that Frank makes sure that Vinnie is held in jail for several days before bail is set, just so that he can cool off. "Personally," he says, "I think you should be taken in for psychological evaluation." Vinnie's proclamation that he's in mourning and that he can't mourn with his family like other people, falls on deaf ears. A deal between them is eventually worked out, however, when it's learned that Zaratzo is responsible for the mutilation and death of a Federal agent. Frank will help Vinnie find out who was responsible for Danny's death, if Vinnie in turn helps him to trap Zaratzo.

Things go according to plan, with Frank picking up a boxer that Danny had had a tussle with over the other man's drug use at the outset of the episode, and driving him around the suburbs of Atlantic City, refusing to allow him a much needed fix. Frank pumps him for information, and eventually learns that Kiki Vanno was responsible.

Meanwhile, Zaratzo is in the midst of clearing his merchandise through customs, when the Federal bust goes down. Vinnie, who's there representing Sonny's interests, is arrested along with everyone else, and thus not held accountable in anybody's—particularly Sonny's—eyes. In fact, when Sonny bails him out later on, he's actually delighted, because he has four million dollars of Zaratzo's, the man is out of the way and any potential heat is off of him.

Vinnie and Sonny approach the limousine, with Sonny telling him to sit up front because he gave the driver the day off. The two of them get in the vehicle, and Sonny starts laughing, telling Vinnie that he's got a special surprise for him because it's his birthday. He slides down the smoked window blocking out the back seat, and Vinnie is stunned to see Kiki Vanno, the man responsible for Danny's death, sitting there with a bullet hole in his forehead, and a ribbon on his chest. Sonny cracks up laughing, and all Vinnie can do is glance back and forth between Kiki's corpse and Sonny's obvious delight at his little "joke." Vengeance is Vinnie's, and the taste is bitter.

"A former writing partner and I had once wanted to do something about boxing," recalls Eric Blakeney. "David had remembered it from our *Crime Story* days and asked me to do it. We worked out a whole new turn on it and I just knocked it off. It was fun, although not terribly complex. My favorite scene is when McPike is driving the junkie around, breaking him down by taking him for a ride through all those nice neighborhoods in Atlantic City. The ending was fun."

Naturally he's speaking of the moment where Sonny lowers the window within the limo, and Vinnie sees his cousin's killer.

"Ken's look was more than 'this guy is nuts,'" Blakeney says. "It's also Vinnie's guilt. He wanted to kill the guy responsible for his cousin's death and Sonny gave him exactly what he wanted. It was Vinnie's confrontation with vengeance. He wasn't really capable of separating himself from it, because all he kept doing was running around saying, 'Hey, I want the guy who killed my cousin and I don't give a shit what I have to do to get him.' And here was the bad guy who delivered it. That was a major growth moment and also a major moment of confusion for Vinnie."

Director Robert Iscove notes, "At that point we weren't worried about reaction, because Steelgrave was so over the top in what he was doing anyway that we felt he could do almost anything. Ken couldn't believe that Sharkey was actually going that far and getting away with it. He was saying, 'Don't you think that's a bit much?' Everyone was saying that Sharkey was so terrific, and Kenny would look at him and say, 'Well, it seems like overacting to me, but, maybe...' and we gradually learned that the style was to go that far with the villains, because then Kenny could react to it and you got the pull."

David Burke felt that "The Birthday Surprise" provided audiences with an opportunity to get to understand the resulting family problems from Vinnie's reputation as a wiseguy.

"That's real important to us," he emphasizes, "because that's what stays with the show, even though we lose the arcs. Vinnie was an outcast from his family because of his mob connections, and we were dealing with how much that hurt him and how painful it was for him. It also showed the human side of him that would use his authority—although some people might say misuse—to deal with his own personal problems, and not be ashamed that he's doing it. So we got to see an emotional side of Vinnie."

"One On One"

Original Air Date 10/15/87

Written by Stephen Kronish

Directed by Ray Villalobos

Guest Starring: Ray Sharkey, Eric Christmas, Dennis Lipscomb, Annette Bening, James Handy and William Bronder

If any episode came close to exposing Vinnie's cover, it was "One On One," in which several of Sonny's carefully laid out plans are disrupted by the arrival of police officers. Vinnie finds himself in the rather unique position of having to discover the inside source, before he himself is exposed as one. His investigation eventually leads to New Jersey police officer Karen LeLand, who has been passing herself off as someone soliciting a donation from Steelgrave Industries for a New Jersey based ballet company. At the same time, she has been sleeping with Syd Royce, who is so taken with Karen that he inadvertently speaks to her about things going on within the company, and/or carelessly discusses them on the telephone while she's in the room.

However, before this is discovered by Vinnie, Syd places a seed of doubt regarding Mr. Terranova firmly in Sonny's mind. This leads to a truly wonderful scene where Sonny questions everyone's loyalty, even Vinnie's, to which he responds by quitting the organization. A little while later, Sonny goes up to the loft, where he finds Vinnie packing his belongings. He tells Vinnie that he's spoken to Syd, to which he responds that Syd is not the problem. It's actually their relationship. "Everything you ask me to do, I do," says Vinnie. "What else do I have to do to convince you, Sonny?" These words obviously leave their mark on Sonny, as he responds that he's fighting for his life. He feels like a piece of beef, and everyone is hacking off their favorite piece: Patrice in New York, Mahoney in Philadelphia, and Syd, the "snake" that's sitting in his brother's office.

Vinnie believes that Syd is going to come down hard on him, and he pleads with Sonny to keep him alive.

"We'll keep each other alive," responds Sonny as he embraces Vinnie lovingly.

The magic of this sequence is that, as Eric Blakeney has stated, you really do get the feeling that Sonny is the *victim* and that Vinnie is wrong for betraying the man's trust.

Despite this scene, there remains some doubt in Sonny's mind, and to satisfy his own burning curiosity he has a few of his people go through Vinnie's belongings, where they discover a series of driver's licenses from various states, including Quantico in Virginia, which just happens to be the place they train Federal agents. In the middle of the night, he phones Vinnie and tells him to get in a limo that's waiting for him downstairs. He does so and in a chilling and effective scene, finds himself sitting with Sonny and one of his people. It's quite obvious that Vinnie is nervous about what's going on, which he chalks up to either a promotion or the fact that he's about to disappear. Sonny calmly—but succinctly—questions him about his driver's license with a Quantico address, and it seems as though he has him cold, until Vinnie makes a "final request" that Sonny give him his wallet. From within it, Vinnie pulls out several pieces of identification with Washington, DC addresses, which he states could imply that maybe Sonny himself has been spending too much time in the nation's capital, where he's been spilling his guts to the justice department and is betraying them all. This seems to provide some satisfaction to Sonny, who suggests that they bring Vinnie back home because he looks tired.

Trying to make amends, Sonny offers him a drink, which Vinnie refuses, wanting to know, instead, what he has to do to convince him. Does he have to kill for him again? Sonny replies that he wants Vinnie to be willing to die for him, to which he says that he nearly does almost every day.

The next night, Vinnie meets Karen at a performance of the ballet, and the two come damn close to a romantic nightcap. Early the following morning, however, Vinnie is stunned to see her leaving Syd's hotel, which he has been staking out. Meanwhile, Syd has constructed another plan to weaken Sonny's foundation of power, by arranging for the police to pick up Harry the Hunch, who's serving as a courier by delivering a quarter of a million dollars. Sonny, once informed, is absolutely convinced that the source came from the inside, and it is Syd who suggests that since the OCB has been harassing him since he opened his casino's doors, they extract the information from Frank McPike and then make him disappear. Sonny disagrees, pointing out that the resulting heat would be too much for them to bear.

Despite instructions to the contrary, from his hotel room Syd arranges for Frank to be picked up so that the information can be extracted, and he states that he wants enough of McPike to be left so that he can inform his fellow agents that "Mr. S." was responsible. Karen, who is lying on the nearby bed, dreading this undercover assignment—has heard it all.

Later, Frank is taken captive to a local laundromat, where the torture begins, as Syd wants him to name anyone he might have on the inside. Elsewhere, Vinnie is informed by Lifeguard that Karen Leland is actually Karen Malloy, and that she's a Jersey cop. He confronts her with this knowledge, revealing his own identity. Getting her to recall conversations Syd had, they come up with the laundromat and rescue Frank, taking out his torturers and finding out that he didn't give up Vinnie's name.

Several days later, the newspaper trumpets the fact that police officer Karen Malloy is missing, and presumed dead. Sonny is relieved to have found his mole at last, and is completely unaware that Syd, having failed to get any other information, discovered she was a cop and had her eliminated, thus avoiding his own incrimination.

That afternoon, alone with Frank, Vinnie needs to know that Karen's disappearance was merely a cover for her hiding by the witness protection program. Frank is sorry to admit that she never showed up; she really did disappear.

Stephen Kronish admits he had a difficult time with the script. "The first draft wasn't very good," he says, "because it was tough for me to get this woman right. She was—and she said this at one point in the script—a whore for the department, and it was kind of tough to get the balance between a woman who would agree to this and an undercover officer. In a sense, she was the flip side of Vinnie Terranova, which came out in the scene between them. I finally worked it out alright, but it took me several passes to get it."

"I think what we were looking for in that episode is that when you're dealing with those crime figures," says David Burke, "undercover people can run into each other and not know it. It also advanced the confrontation between Syd Royce, Vinnie and Steelgrave, and it gave Vinnie a chance to have a relationship with a woman that wasn't especially romantic, but had a touch of it. That was what we were looking to do, while also seeing what kind of illegal activities Steelgrave was involved in that hadn't been considered. We were laying some rope down for that too. It all works together to make it flesh out more realistically. Also, undercover agents frequently are part of illegal activities or bear witness to illegal activities, and it becomes a preponderous of evidence against an individual, as opposed to saying, 'You're under arrest now for this act.' Instead, it becomes a series of acts to demonstrate the length of criminal activity."

"The Prodigal Son"

Original Air Date 10/22/87

Written by Carol Mendelsohn

Directed by Charles Correll

Guest Starring: Ray Sharkey, Elsa Raven, John M. Jackson, Gerald Anthony and Eddie Zammit

The primary storyline of "The Prodigal Son" is that of Vinnie's mother being mugged and his attempt to find the perpetrator. He follows ten dollars stolen from her pocketbook through Chinatown and back into the hands of Sonny Steelgrave. Yet much more is at work here in terms of the relationship of the characters.

First off, Vinnie finally comes to grips with the personal dilemma that has plagued him since the pilot, where his mother believes that he's a gangster. While she's in the hospital suffering from her heart condition after the mugging, he reveals his true identity as a Federal Officer. Frank, of course, is against this, stating that it's a violation of OCB rules, and that such a breach calls for him to be yanked off of his current assignment. This culminates in a reconciliation between mother and son, and Frank is given a choice of alternative tapes he can give to OCB Director Daryl Elias by Lifeguard, who has edited the cassette tape taken from a bug hidden in Mama Terranova's room. In one version, Vinnie reveals his identity; in another, he does not. Frank eventually chooses the latter, showing for the first time in the course of the series that he can be a nice guy.

33

In terms of other relationships, we see Sonny's genuine concern for Vinnie's mom—despite the ongoing struggle between himself and Patrice—sending innumerable flowers to her room, and even coming to see her. In a wonderful scene, she and Sonny are left alone in her hospital room, where she explains that she prefers to pay her own way in this world, although she does appreciate his generosity. She also discusses the death of Sonny's brother, adding that "although no one can replace your brother, someone like Vincenzo might be able to..."

"He already has," Sonny finishes in total sincerity, and it is here that we sense the true depth of the feelings that this man has for Vinnie.

Also interesting is that Vinnie gets to experience first hand what his reputation has done to his old neighborhood's perceptions of him, as everyone he encounters tries to treat him like visiting royalty. The feeling is disconcerting.

David Burke says, "I have a real warm spot in my heart for that episode. I didn't write it, but I had a strong part in blocking it out. The idea of Vinnie's mother being mugged—ripped off for ten bucks—and following that money into the hands of Sonny Steelgrave, was significant. You got to see how a seemingly unrelated act ultimately connects to organized crime, and Vinnie makes the leap that somewhere in this trunk is probably his mother's ten dollars—and he's right. Although he doesn't have any real evidence of it, the audience knows he's right. It also gave Vinnie the chance to tell his mother that he was a cop. After all, what kind of character would have his mother laid up in the hospital with a weak heart who's rejected him because he's a gangster, and not tell her the truth? He *had* to do that."

Eric Blakeney adds that the staff got on "all kinds of wrong tracks with that one. We were really patching it together, although it did come together at the end. The crime in it was crappy, but the emotional aspect of it was nice, especially that the one guy who came to see Vinnie's mother was Sonny, who expressed some nice sentiments. I think mom's flip side of it was a little hokey, with that hammy Italian accent, 'This man is evil!' I think that's bullshit. I would have liked Vinnie's mom, rather than be able to be a great actor, to have seen the lost boy in Sonny as opposed to pretending to see it. Obviously Sonny is a lonely man who has no family left. He has a lot of love in him that's been misplaced, and he's a spoiled, confused and lost child. The show had some terrific moments in it, I just don't think that structurally we were able to set up everything the way we should have.

"The episode also provided a real good look at Sonny and what kind of person he was. When Vinnie's mother was in the hospital, Sonny's attitude was, 'Everything stops. We go and help your mom.' That was really a major moment in their relationship, which led to Vinnie's confusion and emotional turmoil. Those aspects of it were really terrific."

"A Deal's A Deal"

Original Air Date 10/29/87

Written by David J. Burke and Stephen Kronish

Directed by Charles Correll

Guest Starring: Ray Sharkey, Joe Dallesandro, Billy Vera, Dan Lauria, Steve Vinovich, Joe Shea, Nathan Davis and Martina Finch

A self-proclaimed rock and roll dinosaur, singer Joey Romanowski, now in his forties, finally has a hit record on his hands, and he wants to take full advantage of it by making the rounds in a tour that will earn him upwards of a million dollars. The problem is that he's under contract to Sonny Steelgrave, who wants him to continue playing the Jersey circuit and will not allow him to tour. Vinnie tries to make Joey's case, but his pleas fall on deaf ears, as Sonny is in no mood to be benevolent. Out of desperation, Joey goes to Mahoney, asking for help to get out of his contract. Mahoney says he'll do what he can.

Suddenly we're back in Sonny's office, and Mahoney is shouting at Sonny, telling him that he's going to lose everything if he doesn't get a firmer grip and that the situation with Joey is a perfect example. Patrice is going to move in and make total claim to the Atlantic City territory unless he does something about it now. Sonny hears these words, and it seems that all the pain and power slippage he's felt over the last few months are going to be taken out on Joey, who he wants a lesson taught to. Then, during their conversation, a package is delivered. Sonny opens it up and finds that it contains a limited edition rifle that Dave had ordered for Sonny's birthday prior to his death. He's extremely moved by this gesture, and it has the effect of beginning a feeling of loss in his life that would be dealt with in much greater detail during the next episode. As a result, he gets together with don Baglia, his wife and their daughter, Theresa, and the attraction between these old friends is instantly obvious.

Meanwhile, a pair of cops on the Steelgrave payroll are sent out to rough Joey up, but one of them gets too zealous and crushes the singer's larynx, thus effectively ending his career. Joey is brought to the hospital and Frank, after realizing that the crooked cops on the Steelgrave payroll coupled with testimony from Joey would be enough to get Steelgrave, begins to investigate the case. The cops, fearful of discovery, begin tailing Frank, and take photos of him with Vinnie when the two men meet. These photos, they reason, would be worth plenty to Sonny, particularly when they discover who it is that's in the photos with McPike.

It all culminates that night at a ceremony Don Baglia has insisted on in which Vinnie is inducted into La Familia, an event attended by, among others, Mahoney and Patrice. One of the cops tries to exchange the photos with Sonny for money, but Joey, seeking revenge for what's happened, blows him away. Next he turns his weapon on Sonny, but before he can pull the trigger, Frank has no choice but to shoot him. At the same time, the envelope of photos that were to be given to Sonny end up at his feet. He's about to pick it up, when Frank grabs them, puts them in his jacket pocket and presses his gun against Steelgrave, pushing him back. Frank starts to walk away, when Sonny's lawyer stops him, demanding that the property be returned to Sonny. Frank considers this, removes an envelope, hands it to the lawyer and leaves. What Sonny has been given are doctored photos of Frank with Patrice, thus Vinnie's ass has been saved once again.

"A Deal's A Deal" owes more than a passing nod to Ray Sharkey's big screen vehicle *The Idolmaker*. It is interesting in that it sets up Sonny's morose over his life and dreams of the future, while introducing the Baglia family as a dramatic element. In many ways, though, it feels like an inserted episode, which it was, since it was shot *after* the final episode of the arc in which the character of Sonny Steelgrave died. One thing is missing, and it's an element that should have been carried over from "The Prodigal Son," is the new level of friendship that Vinnie and Sonny had moved to after his obvious regard for Vinnie's mother.

"I love 'A Deal's A Deal'," enthuses David Burke. "I wrote it with Steve Kronish over a weekend, and it was the last one we shot of that arc, because the network was so in love with Sonny Steelgrave's relationship with Vinnie Terranova that they wanted to keep him around for another episode. It was a show that had to be very confined, and it was a chance to introduce Don Baglia, his daughter and served as a lead to the next episode in terms of Sonny's getting married. It also gave us a sense of Sonny's family, because this gun arrives that his brother had ordered for him prior to his death. That was important, and so was the scene where Don Baglia would be hurt if Vinnie isn't inducted into the family in the old way.

Sonny doesn't want to do it, but he also doesn't want to offend don Baglia, so he goes through with it. All of it was good character stuff."

Stephen Kronish adds, "It was not actually supposed to be done. We hadn't planned to do that show. It was an extra Sonny Steelgrave episode, and I think the most difficult thing about it was that it was shot after the episode that ended Sonny Steelgrave. It was tough for us, but a lot tougher for the the crew, and particularly Ken and Ray, because they had just come off this tremendous emotional peak and now had to get it up again for this episode. It was a very tough, emotional period for them and for us, because we knew we were taking a tremendous risk. Here we were, working on the Steelgrave arc, which was so good and the relationship between them was working so well and it was so unique, and we were getting rid of it. Also, we were going into an arc [Mel and Susan Profitt] where we had real concerns about the lack of emotional connection between Vinnie and the people he was investigating, where these people were so diametrically opposed to Vinnie Terranova. At least with Sonny Steelgrave, Sonny and Vinnie were very much the same, but there was nothing similar about Mel Profitt. So we as the writing staff were having a very hard time readjusting ourselves. When we were ending that arc, we felt like we were losing a member of the family, and yet we knew we had to do it. We were also not sure where we were going to go, and how that was going to work, all of which made 'A Deal's A Deal' that much harder for us to handle."

Although Eric Blakeney enjoyed the idea of doing an additional Steelgrave episode, he hated the primary motivation of "A Deal's A Deal."

"It was tough because we'd gone through the emotion of Sonny already dying. Everybody was kind of not there," he says. "As a matter of fact, Kenny and Ray really wanted to do a show more on the emotional bonding between them. They were really in conflict with David and Steve Kronish about the content of the episode. They wanted to show these guys just bonding together, feeling that it would really add to the tragedy of the climax, and they were right. Kenny and Ray had become very tight. Ray describes the moment when he puts his hand in the electric box, saying, 'It was eerie, man.' Everyone on the crew was affected by it, and nobody's heart was in this episode.

"I remember when I came on the series," Blakeney continues, "one of the things they said was, 'Listen, we have a real dilemma here in that Sharkey is so incredible. He's the bad guy, and we're going to lose our series to the villain. What we've got to remember is that every now and then he has to pull the limo over and "kick the dog".' My reaction to that was that it was exactly what we *shouldn't* do. I just made a huge pain in the ass of myself by insisting that the real great part of the series is having him pull the limo over, get out and *pet* the dog. That's what was working for us. We did episodes to prove that Ray was the bad guy, simply because everyone was terrified that once Ray went down, we would lose the series. 'A Deal's A Deal' is the episode where he symbolically got out of the limo and kicked the dog. The whole purpose of the episode, which I thought was one of the worst episodes I've ever seen, was to show that this man is 'pure evil.' I had to do some of the rewriting and some of the tweaks on that. It was a grim labor for me. I'd really fallen in love with what we were doing there, and I felt that there were tremendous opportunities in developing that relationship further."

And what was Ray Sharkey's reaction to a "kick the dog" episode?

"I have a knack of kicking the dog and making you feel sorry for *me*," he laughs. "That's what acting is all about. I was constantly getting that, but, listen, there was nothing they could do to get me to perform it a different way. It's not that I was stubborn, but that's just the way it was happening existentially. Hindsight, everybody's a genius. While we were doing it, everybody's just doing the best they could. I guess the funniest thing [about 'A Deal's A Deal'] is that they shot [it] about a week after my death scene, and the joke was that we were shooting a ghost. I was not Sonny anymore. I was Ray. Sonny was dead, for all of us. We all watched him die, and it was really insane."

"The Marriage of Heaven and Hell"

Original Air Date 11/5/87

Written by Eric Blakeney

Directed by Zale Dalen

Guest Starring: Ray Sharkey, Joe Dallesandro, Eric Christmas, Dennis Lipscomb, Nathan Davis, Robert Mangiardi, Martina Finch, Elsa Raven and Joe Shea

Depressed because he's feeling his own mortality, Sonny confesses his love for Theresa Baglia and proposes to her. She accepts and plans are put into effect for their marriage to take place. Meanwhile, Vinnie and Sonny have conspired to have a public falling out, to see if Patrice tries to recruit him, which, of course, he does after Syd Royce reports the fact that Terranova is "seducible."

Beneath all of this, preparations are being made for a war between the families. By marrying Theresa, Sonny is essentially aligning himself with the Baglia family as well as their connections, and that's something Patrice, who wants to claim Atlantic City as his own, can't afford.

Later, Vinnie, who's been approached by Patrice, tells Sonny about their conversation, and the fact that it looks like Mahoney is in cahoots. Sonny in turn tells him his plan: to ask Pat the Cat to be his best man, just so that he can keep an eye on him. To this end, he and Vinnie meet with Patrice, where Sonny asks him, and the man acts as though it's the greatest thrill of his life. Later still, Vinnie meets with Patrice in a bar, stating that he's very unhappy where he currently is. Patrice offers to pay him even more than Sonny has been, and explains that the plan is to murder Sonny on the morning of his wedding. He needs Vinnie to get a layout of the hall and to smuggle weapons. He says it will be done, and departs. Patrice goes back to his table, where we see him talking to Aldo Baglia, Sonny's future brother-in-law, telling him that once Sonny's been taken care of, he wants Terranova killed as well. "I hate a traitor," he says.

Vinnie goes to Frank and tells him about the meeting, and Frank says that he can't say anything to Sonny about the hit. Vinnie ultimately agrees to this, adding that if Frank isn't there on time, he's going to stop it himself—he will not allow Sonny to be murdered. Frank agrees, adding that there will be a twelve hour video deck in the room to record everything that goes on.

Then Vinnie goes to see his mother in Brooklyn, and they have a conversation about the guilt that he is feeling in bringing down his friend. His mother asks if he cares for this man, to which he replies in the affirmative. She calls him a fool, and he is stunned by her words. "Vincenzo," she says, "what good is a man who loves his children, but kills somebody else's?" These words seem to have an impact on him.

At Sonny's bachelor party that night, things take a surprising turn, beginning at the point where Sonny delivers the following speech that epitomizes the mortality he has been feeling as of late, as well as his resolve for the future:

"All my life I've been chasing a taste of something that could make me feel more alive," he says. "Some kind of magic fumes....that I could breathe in and fill my soul. Something that I could feel pumping in my blood. I've tried everything, except making new life. That's why I'm here, to make new life to keep me alive, forever. I think man was born hungry. He spends his life hunting, trying to satisfy that hunger. We hunt more and more, trying to find something that will make us feel fuller. That emptiness...it's always there. It comes from isolation. A man who is isolated, is empty!"

And with that, he strangles Patrice to death, which sends Syd Royce into a state of shock and tears. One of Patrice's men gets up, but Aldo moves in quickly, and shoots him while Mahoney just sits there, serving as proof that both of them had informed Sonny of Patrice's plan. Sonny extends his hand, asking them who will join his family. Vinnie, whose expressions betray his horror, is the first to stand.

Patrice's body is loaded into a large ice chest, and the party continues as though nothing had ever happened. Next morning, everyone retires to their rooms with hookers that Mahoney had hired for the evening. Only Sonny and Vinnie are left behind, and the episode concludes with Sonny asking one very simple question: "Hey, Vinnie. Why didn't you tell me Patrice was going to hit me?"

The entire last act of "The Marriage of Heaven and Hell" is quite powerful, elevating Sonny's character to a new level. On the one hand, it's gruesome to actually see him murder someone with his own hands, while at the same token it is something you feel you have to applaud, because, once again, he was being made a victim.

"'The Marriage of Heaven and Hell' was Sonny trying to get rid of Pat 'the cat' Patrice," says David Burke. "You don't know it in that episode until the very end, but he's in cohoots with Mahoney, and he's keeping it from Vinnie too that he's set up this whole scheme to get rid of his main threat. That episode was very dark, very strong, very powerful and, really, the first half of a tour de force. The death [of Patrice] has been likened to *The Untouchables*, and maybe that's true, but for Sonny to do it in a room full of people, and then to throw the body in an ice chest, he couldn't have more disdain for the guy."

Eric Blakeney, the writer of part one, accepts the comparison to that Brian De Palma film, while pointing out some significant differences.

"Not to dump on David Mamet," he says, referring to the screenwriter of *The Untouchables*, "but he was just being clever about execution. It was a real clever rap about baseball, but the scene was about murder. Our scene was about murder as well, but it was also about what this guy was going through, and what he was saying was that he was afraid of dying. The only way he could see to become immortal was to create new life. He had reached a point where his life was simply empty. It was a terrible tragedy. This man was growing tremendously, but unfortunately he had to pay for his crimes, because he was a complete person in his range of emotions and what he was feeling, but he didn't put it together on how to behave in society. That's what the speech was about. I knew the comparisons to *The Untouchables* would be there, and my attitude was, 'Just *listen* to what he's saying.'

"Also, the whole idea of this as well is that Vinnie was in complete turmoil, chaos and confusion with what he was feeling in that scene where he goes to his mother and says, 'My best friend is the man I'm going to bring down, and I don't feel good about it. It has a bad taste. What I'm doing is technically correct, and right by the law, but on a personal level it stinks.' And she tells him that everybody can be nice. If you went to a dinner party thrown by Hitler, I'm sure he was a very charming host, but the guy killed six million Jews. That's where you've got to measure a human being. You'll find something admirable in everyone. It's all in degrees. Where you decide to draw the line is an individual choice, and it's also a choice that society makes in where it draws the line in terms of accepted behavior. She's basically saying, 'I'm sure he's a great guy and there's no question that he loves you, but he kills people; he's an evil man.' It is that moment, and having Patrice murdered right there, that had to be done in Vinnie's face. I loathed making it look like *The Untouchables*, but I needed the combination. I couldn't have him just kill in his face. He had to have that thing where you see that this is a man who's afraid of dying; that this is a vulnerable, tragic man who loves and needs to be loved, but who kills. That was the wake-up call for Vinnie to do his job—the moment for Vinnie where he sees that. Remember, he was even telling McPike, 'I'm not letting those guys kill him. No matter what happens!' He was basically saying he loved the guy, even though he knows he has to bring him down.

"As a dramatist, that's the kind of conflict you really wish for, especially in the land of Hollywood, because you usually don't get it. Emotionally, you're faced with writing episodes for shows like *Hunter*, where you just go out and catch evil-doers every week. There's no conflict. You can't call the threat of bent noses with uzis a conflict, because they're not going to kill you. This had true conflict for him. Those moments all through the climax, where he draws the line between right and wrong, and that the person he loves falls below that line. That was the moment for Vinnie where he realizes he's got to do his job, because prior to that he was actually moving to a point where he might not be able to.

"The whole thing works much better as a two hour movie rather than two individual episodes. It starts in a small but complexly political manner, and everything looks innocent. They're just going to this little church in the Bronx, but it's a meeting of evil. It just escalates from there. The two part was modeled on all the betrayals and intrigues of *The House of Caesars*, and that's one of the areas, had we coordinated it better, I think we could have made a little more interesting with a little more intrigue. I would have liked to have coordinated both parts a little better. I think thematically we were connected, but there were parts where it drifted apart a little bit. We didn't communicate as well on the final stages and really write it as one piece together. When David said we were going to kill Sharkey, even though I didn't want to kill him, I knew instantly how I wanted to do it. When I laid it on the guys, they just loved it and we took it from there."

"No One Gets Out of Here Alive"

Original Air Date 11/12/87

Written by David J. Burke

Directed by Robert Iscove

Guest Starring: Ray Sharkey, Eric Christmas, Dennis Lipscomb, Nathan Davis, Robert Mangiardi, John M. Jackson, Martina Finch, Joe Shea and Richard Donat

While Sonny says Vinnie is his Judas, Aldo Baglia enters the room to remove Patrice's body from the ice chest, so he can "bury it deep." Knowing that Vinnie has betrayed Sonny, Aldo asks him if he needs his gun, to which he responds in the negative. Aldo takes off with his "cargo". Sonny, who simply can't believe that Vinnie would betray him for the likes of Patrice, tells him that he's going to let him live, this way he'll always have to watch his shadows, never knowing when his last day of life will be.

A short while later the phone rings. It's Aldo, calling from the car, and informing Sonny that he just passed over a dozen police cars headed their way. This catches Sonny by surprise, but then he puts it all together, turns to Vinnie and says matter of factly, "You're a cop!"

What essentially follows is a car chase to a movie theatre just closing for the season, in which they are locked. There they get involved in a violent fist fight, resulting in both being bloodied and nearly unconscious. When they get to their feet, they find that there's no place to go. Sonny proceeds to break into the theater's bar, and begins drinking, as he and Vinnie verbally assault each other, and then sink into a simple conversation, every word tainted. Then silence descends on them as the highly appropriate "Nights in White Satin" begins playing on the jukebox.

As Frank and the other cops arrive and start breaking the theatre door down, Vinnie and Sonny have a last conversation that sums up the nature of their relationship, as Sonny is still convinced that he can beat the justice system.

VINNIE: "I want you to know that there's a lot about who you are that I feel close to....You stupid bastard. I had my men rocking in there at 7:00 this morning, plenty of time to keep Patrice from killing you. You were going to be the *victim*, Sonny. I dealt you the best hand I could. I was giving you a position from which you could negotiate, but you screwed up, man. You had to indulge your bloodlust."

SONNY: "This is it. What am I looking at?....You a Federal or Jersey cop? I can't believe you're a cop! Either way it's conspiracy. What am I looking at? I can grow tomatoes with former Wall Street wizards. Me and Ivan Boesky. He did time, didn't he? Yeah, he did time. I can make this work for me. I can make a much stronger case. I can plead down to a year, maybe eighteen months worse case. They'll try to extract a price from me, but they're too smart to take it to court. Jurors don't believe liars. You're a liar, and, my pal, you are a major league liar. You've been lying for years. You don't even know what the truth is anymore."

VINNIE: "What about what you did to Patrice?"

SONNY: "You're going to tell them about that? What about all those feelings you said you had for me?"

VINNIE: "Sonny, I feel for you deeply, but you can't run from this murder."

SONNY: "Patrice is gone, man. He's gone forever. They got no corpse, they got no case."

VINNIE: "They got video tape. [The camera] was in the ceiling in the ballroom. It was hooked up to a twelve hour deck."

SONNY: "You know what the penalty in this state is? Lethal injection. They strap you to a gurney and pump you full of morphine. Half the officials in the state watch it on close circuit TV. You'd like that, wouldn't you? You know, half those guys watching me slip into oblivion are on my payroll, like you. How much of my money do you have in the bank, Vinnie? What do you get out of this? Another pin on your lapel? An upgrade on your pension? Why are you trying to destroy me, man?"

VINNIE: "It comes with the territory, Sonny. You want [a list]? How about drugs killing kids and fraud destroying pensioners."

SONNY: "Oh my God. Who do you think you're working for? You want to talk drugs? Let's talk Agent Orange. Let's talk LSD. Those are just two progressive efforts made on behalf of your friendly employer, Uncle Sam. You want to talk fraud? Let's talk fraud. Why don't you try explaining to a farmer why the Federal guarantee loans are being recalled. You're the mob in this room, Vinnie."

VINNIE: "I saw you garotte a man in my face!"

SONNY: "I'd do it again, but I'd do it myself. I don't have to send teenagers off to the slaughter and the next day make excuses for it in the Op Ed page. You have no idea what this is about, do you, man? This is about taxes. Money. They don't like that I don't want to pay what they think is my share. My legal operations pay more than half the major corporations in this country."

VINNIE: "This is not about taxes."

SONNY: "Then what's it about?"

VINNIE: "This is about the core of yourself that cannot be excused by whatever it is about you I admire. This is about the need in your life not to run rampant over other people's lives simply because your fire burns brighter. Hey, this is about the law, man!"

SONNY: "I loved you, man!"

And with that, Sonny plunges his hand into an electrical panel, thus electrocuting himself just as McPike and the others get through the door. Vinnie screams out Sonny's name, but to no avail. Frank, in perhaps the most emotional state we've ever seen him, tries to provide consolation, his voice breaking, stating that Vinnie should be proud of himself because he didn't give in to the enticement of power as many people would have. The words have little impact on him, as he is read his rights and led to a waiting squad car in order to keep his cover intact, the words of "Night in White Satin" echoing in his mind. The saga of Sonny Steelgrave is over.

"I think that one of the best episodes of television I've ever seen was this one," enthuses Stephen Kronish. "It also spoke very much to the strength of the idea of an arc, because you couldn't do that show as a single episode. It would have none of the impact that we had built up over the course of nine episodes. It was just tremendous, and one of the few times that I think everything came together perfectly. The script was great, the direction was great, the performances were great and everything that you wanted to work, worked. That happens very rarely."

Says David Burke, "That's the show I'm proudest of. I swung for the fences on that one and got a home run. That episode was very satisfying for everybody and it felt real good to do. Actually, it was a story that I had wanted to do for years, and these two characters just worked for it. I had an outline I had done about a bookie and a guy who owed him money, who is basically a middle-class guy. The bookie's wife is bugging him to bring home a little more bacon, the bookie finds himself chasing this guy and they end up locked in a theatre. So here were my two guys, and I could play it out to a different conclusion. The story was already set, and I only had to work these characters into it.

"I knew Sonny was going to go in that episode, and the last thing I wanted to do was have a fire fight. It seemed to me that the best way to see Sonny off was to lock these two guys in a room together, beat each other senseless physically and tear each other down to their roots emotionally. It was as simple as trying to do that, and leaving the audience understanding Sonny's justification for his behavior, and almost buying into it when he gives his speech to Vinnie. A lot of people who have watched that scene, thought Sonny was right and he was, but it didn't justify his antisocial behavior. It was certainly the most emotional episode we ever did, and it remains a favorite of a lot of people."

Eric Blakeney recalls, "David and I were writing in my car. I put 'Good Lovin'' on and I said, 'Let's have a scene where they're trapped in this place together that has a jukebox, and let's have music connect them up on boyhood memories. Now 'Good Lovin' worked perfectly for me, but 'Nights in White Satin'? There's no way in hell Sonny Steelgrave would have been into that song, so I didn't...I love the song, but I thought at that moment which consists of close-ups of the two guys, there were things that could have been said between them which weren't, and it frustrated the shit out of me. First of all, Ray started on something with this whole thing about his memories of 'Good Lovin' and unhooking his first bra, which was great, but when he looks at Vinnie when 'Nights in White Satin' came on, they just played these looks between two lovers. But there was something incredibly powerful in the continuation of the thought 'I love you, but you're going to take my life away.' I didn't feel that Vinnie got enough of Sonny confronting him on his betrayal, and that it was handled kind of cursory. They were really just hammering home the point, 'You broke the law, and now you have to pay.' I felt that a lot of it was good, because the law is the law, but there were moments in there that weren't wholly honest for me.

"I think when somebody you love is going to end your life, there's something incredibly powerful in being face to face and going with that thought, which I don't think we really hit. If you thought that was incredibly emotional, I think in terms of what we *could* have gotten out of it emotionally, and I don't think we even got close. I thought the potential really went untapped. I know Ray and Rob Iscove had some really good ideas about what they wanted to do with that confrontation, and I thought his whole rap about the government wasn't really the thing. That's not what it was about for Ray. It wasn't about explaining the government was full of shit, it's about what's going on there between the two of them, and although it was mentioned, it was never fully attacked. A great moment is when he killed himself, which is incredibly powerful. I really think David did a great job with that. I just think it would have been the most devastating moment in television if we had turned it up a notch. I would have lost some of the cleverness and just boiled it down to the two of them face to face, and really hammered home that emotion. In that moment in the previous episode where Vinnie realizes that this guy is a murderer and he can do his job, it seemed as though his purpose was clear all through the final part. He was able to say, 'Of course I love this guy, but he's evil, and I have to do my job.' As a piece of drama, I don't think that the conflict ever became too much for Vinnie.

"That bothered me. I would like to have seen Kenny take one more added turn. I think that's all it would have taken to do it, if we could have questioned at one point in that hour whether or not he could go through with it. I don't think there was ever that question. Every episode was leading up to that point. When the moment comes, are you going to be able to bring this guy down? In the whole second part, I felt that there was no question about it. I'm just being incredibly picky, because it was a really spectacular episode, but I'm a dramatist, and if there's a little more conflict to be gotten, I want it."

Director Robert Iscove has his own distinct memories of that final episode. "When I went into the theatre on that one," he recalls, "I said, 'Okay, we're going to do 'Good Lovin'' and I want to break all the stuff behind the bar.' Well, the calls that went back and forth to LA. 'You want to do what? Why do you want to smash stuff? He's supposed to be dancing around.' I said, 'Because this guy's not going to dance at that point. He's going to do something else, so I'm going to have him break everything in the place. And then you pull back to the absolute quiet of 'Nights in White Satin.' The other way, the contrast didn't seem as effective to me, especially after we'd come off of that huge fight. Where do you escalate the violence to or what's the next twist to the relationship? Ray's death scene was an emotional one for all of us, and so was the subsequent scene between Kenny and Jonathan. We actually did that pretty much in sequence, so we had done the other stuff inside and it was two in the morning, and we were all emotional wrecks. But 'Nights in White Satin' was the high point emotionally, because you see the love these two guys had for each other."

Interestingly, there was a tremendous amount of debate behind the scenes of **Wiseguy** regarding the fate of Sonny Steelgrave, with many of those involved wanting actor Ray Sharkey to survive the entire first season.

"Getting rid of Sharkey was a decision that David had made," explains Eric Blakeney, "because he wanted to move on to something else, but there were many more complexities of the Vinnie/Sonny relationship we wanted to explore. There were two pieces I was using to model Steelgrave on, *Gilgamesh* and *The Twelve Caesars*, although it was mostly *Gilgamesh*. Generally, the growth and complexities were never fully explored. There were more politics to be involved in the Steelgrave arc, because you're setting up the structure of a kingdom and there was much more to explore in that kingdom. Vinnie's connection to it, Sonny's connection and how they intertwine. There was just a lot more for us to borrow from. I would have probably done more with Sonny's relationship with Theresa Baglia's family and more with Vinnie's roots in Brooklyn, where the family is. I think the more that relationship bonded and became complex, the more explosive the finale would have been."

David Burke doesn't agree. "I had worked on *Crime Story*," he says, "where extending the conflict between the hero and the villain really hurt the show. To extend that storyline would have been to diminish Vinnie as a character, and he was the star of the show. If we had stayed with Steelgrave, Vinnie would have had to leave the OCB and become a hood, which would certainly change the show. I think one of the biggest problems with *Crime Story* was that they didn't catch Ray Luca. How effective could this cop have been, if he couldn't catch one villain? I thought we would be repeating what was a very bad mistake."

"Last Rites For Lucci"

Original Air Date 11/19/87

Written by Stephen Kronish

Directed by Bill Corcoran

Guest Starring: James Andronica, Gerald Anthony, Ricardo Gutierrez, Matt Landers and Jon Slade

The remnants of the Vinnie/Sonny relationship surfaced in "Last Rites For Lucci," which is technically the final part of the Steelgrave arc, examining the aftermath of Vinnie's "betrayal." Through the course of the episode, we see Vinnie struggling with the demons of his mind as he tries to come to grips with what he's just been through. The OCB orders him into a group therapy program, and at first he is resistant to open up to these people who have gone through similar experiences. He does, however, hook up with Mike Stowiecki, an angry cop who is living on the edge. Ultimately the pressure becomes too much for Stowiecki, resulting in his killing himself. Vinnie is forced to wonder whether or not this is a fate that may be awaiting him as well.

Between all this, Vinnie discovers through his brother Pete that old friend Nick Lucci has had a contract put out on him by a politician who has been heavily involved with kickbacks. Time is running out for Lucci, and it really comes down to Vinnie helping him out of this jam and quite literally saving his life.

"'Last Rites For Lucci' got Vinnie back to the neighborhood," says Stephen Kronish, "and I liked the fact that we got into it sort of backwards; that Vinnie was helping an old buddy. I think Ken also did a great job playing those therapy scenes. I had done some research with a guy who was the head psychologist for the LAPD in terms of what these guys do go through—that period of separation and the feeling of betrayal."

David Burke adds, "That show was a natural progression for Vinnie. His first undercover assignment had been so successful, but he had gotten so close to his target as well. How these men have to deal with these problems was something that was of interest to us. It just seemed a natural place to go, rather than have him leap right into another case."

Eric Blakeney explains, "I think Steve did a really excellent job with the ghosts of guilt haunting Vinnie. It wasn't easy. He couldn't just do his job and not be affected by it. The series at that point was about the seepage into a man's psyche when he goes undercover, because they lose their marbles. The whole idea of living something 24 hours a day can affect a man who's among the greatest of heroes, and that vulnerability in his position was making the show so great. It was like, 'My God, this guy is crumbling on us. He can't handle this. This is too much.' I felt that from that point on, it was never too much for him. He may not have liked the job and he may not have liked the people, but because it was so much easier to see who the bad guys and who the good guys were, it made his job easier and I think the series suffered for it."

While **Wiseguy** would never quite match the emotional scale of the Steelgrave arc (although the rag trade storyline would come close), the cast and crew tried with all their abilities and creativity, resulting in a creativity that is still head and shoulders above most television crime dramas.

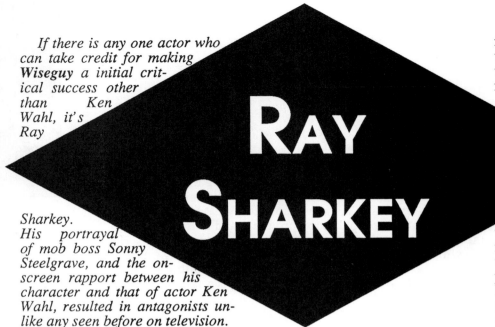

RAY SHARKEY

If there is any one actor who can take credit for making **Wiseguy** *a initial critical success other than Ken Wahl, it's Ray Sharkey.*

His portrayal of mob boss Sonny Steelgrave, and the on-screen rapport between his character and that of actor Ken Wahl, resulted in antagonists unlike any seen before on television.

Sharkey had scored very successfully with small feature roles and then in 1981's The Idolmaker, *before succumbing to the trappings of stardom and a well publicized bout with drugs and alcohol. Now, since his portrayal of Steelgrave, he has been on something of a roll, starring in a variety of motion pictures, including* Wired *and* Scenes From the Class Struggle in Beverly Hills, *NBC's* The Revenge of Al Capone, *The Showtime miniseries* The Neon Empire *and is currently prepping an ABC private eye series, which is to be executive produced by Eric Blakeney,* **Wiseguy***'s first season story editor.*

As can be discerned from the following, Sharkey obviously holds his tenure as Sonny Steelgrave in high regard, speaking enthusiastically of the behind the scenes atmosphere on the show.

The chemistry between me and Kenny, put together with the dialogue from Eric, David—all the guys, loaned itself to what was happening. Also, any director that would come up would see this on the first day of shooting, and get really excited and stretch themselves a little farther. And production stretched themselves for us...a lot. They went the extra mile for us, because they saw what was happening and they weren't pulling the plug after fourteen hours.

They were giving us that extra half hour to shoot that extra take of that extra scene, and everybody was in to it.

We could not have had a better place in time to do it, because everybody on the crew, from the craft serviceman to the people in production in the office, would all come to the set to watch the scenes being played. And then the screening rooms in LA were packed, because they wanted to see it. It was really special. Kenny and I were just going at it. We were having a good time, we knew something was up and we knew it wasn't going to last a long time, so we just continued to do what we were doing. In fact, one interesting thing that happened is that when we were shooting the last episode, that was one of the worst weeks in Vancouver. We all knew that Sonny was leaving, and for me, too, it was really gut-wrenching. I had made a deal to make this movie, and I couldn't get any farther away from Vancouver than Greece, you know what I mean? I had already made the deal, and it was really solemn. The vibes were thick.

We started to shoot the last episode, and every hour it would get better and better and better. Specifically what happened is that we shot the last part first. We shot all the exteriors, the chase sequences in the cars, and then we went into the theatre and we stayed in the theatre for five days. We used different parts of the theatre for different sections of the episode, so what we did was shoot all the end stuff first, because it was easier to shoot it there. The wild thing is that everybody would come into the theatre, take their seats and watch this play. We were covering it from a lot of different angles, because it was so well written that no matter how we played it, it got better and better. Naturally when that happens, you shoot the shit out of it, which was what was happening take after take after take. And then this funny thing happened. They had to shoot my death, and naturally I had this stunt guy go and get electrocuted and I had to do the close-up. I actually watched myself die. It was really, really strange and really bizarre. Everybody in the crew started crying, and it was really heavy. It was over.

The funny thing that happened is that they wanted an extra episode, so they had to shoot an extra episode the following week and the joke was that we were shooting a ghost. I was not Sonny anymore. I was Ray. Sonny was dead, for all of us. We all watched him die, and it was really insane.

The other thing that happened, is when we shot "Good Lovin'" We had a director named Rob Iscove, and Robbie was a dancer and choreographer, and I being a dancer and a singer, it lent itself to what we did. We didn't have anything laid out on paper, but we would go to the specific sections of the song and set and say, "Okay, let's break it up into four bars each shot," and I'd say, "I'm going to face that way." We didn't know what we were going to do, but they would roll the camera, roll the song and I would destroy and do whatever in one section of the place and move on to other sections, and really wing it until we had it all together. It was really wild. Nobody had ever done it like that before. That's insane to do that and get away with it, but we were on such a roll at that point.

It had come from Eric Blakeney's show, "The Marriage of Heaven and Hell," and what had happened is that the show went on as usual, but the last fifteen minutes of the show was the bachelor party, and the day after the bachelor party we started shooting the second half. That night we spent the whole day shooting the bachelor party, which you never hear of in television. Even Cannell came up, sat at the top of a ladder so he could see the whole thing. Everybody was there, and I remember doing that speech in one take, and we moved on. By the end of the night we were in a lot of trouble. Everybody was in overtime, but nobody cared. Steven Cannell gave this great speech from on top of the ladder, "There's magic happening here tonight, and I want to thank you guys for what you've done for me and what we've done for each other." He gave this great speech like "Go ahead, knock yourselves out," and everybody was into it. We had a young Canadian crew and they really got spoiled. Even I got spoiled. Rarely in my life do those things happen; rarely are you on the set and looking in the eyes of the crew, and you're aware of what's happening. Needless to say, it took about six months for me to finally separate from everybody. We were all calling each other all the time. I had not had the opportunity to see the episodes because I was away. I called Kenny and everybody and found out that the show was great.

I really didn't realize the power that it had until I got back into America, because I was travelling around and everybody was like, "Good morning, Mr. Steelgrave." I remember arriving in the New York airport, and people went nuts over me. I was turning around to see who they were goggling over. When the reruns came on, it was even worse. Boxes of mail arrived at the office addressed to me. It was insane, and crazy time. I

thought, "Wow, we really must have done it," and it's been wild ever since.

Half the people who are fans caught it on the reruns. CBS put me on this promo tour, which was unprecedented. Nobody ever went on a promo tour for reruns, but the mail was so incredible that we went out and did this tour and people were giving us these Sonnyisms. I was in Brooklyn over the summer, and I had this guy come up to me...I always have people come up and they're always big fans, they know this and they know that, but this guy knew every line of every show. I'm telling you, I was impressed. He did Sonny better than I did. He knew every line, and I mean obscure lines, he knew all of Vinnie and Sonny's dialogue.

One thing that happened is that Kenny and I worked so closely together that he knew all of my lines and I knew all of his. So we would do impressions of each other of what we did because we didn't get a chance to watch dailies. We would start doing each other's lines from different episodes, and we would play a game in which we would try to guess what episode the dialogue was coming from. What you really wanted to see was Ray Sharkey doing Vinnie Terranova and Ken Wahl doing Sonny Steelgrave. Then we transcended that, and took it to another level. This is something that has to be in the book, because it wasn't on film. We were having such a good time and our creative juices were flowing, and in between takes we created these two

old guys named Archie and Sam. They were really Sonny and Vinnie, but they were like 90 years old, and they farted all the time, had bad manners, loved tits and ass, you know, those kind of guys. They were stuck in an old actor's home, where they would discuss their days in Vancouver on **Wiseguy**. Those were the *real* interesting guys.

I got an award from the Viewers for Quality Television, and it was unprecedented. I look back at it now, and it's really very simple. That's part of the reason that I've got Eric Blakeney on my new show, because I understand that these guys understood the guys they were writing about, which was about the human dilemma. They were writing about themes that came out of *The Bible* that were very simple. That's the truth, you know. They would take things out of the bible, and Eric would says, "Well, this is Caesar's arc, this is the Caesar week," or this is Jacob's week or Job's week. And he really would use very simple dilemmas in terms of betrayal, honor, honesty, just real simple things that happened between men and men or men and women. And it all worked for us, because no matter what happened in the scope of things, Vinnie Terranova was a liar, and he was brought up not to be a liar. Here he meets this man, and they fall in love with each other because of their common denominator: morality. When people become friends, it's like an unwritten law that they know that, morally, they're the same person. They know that they would not cross that line, and there really isn't a price that they are willing to pay; that they're not for sale, and that makes a bond for friendship. I think we played with that bond every week. We tried to figure out how far we could take it, and the reason the last two episodes were so powerful is that we took it to the limit. *Betrayal*.

That's what made it work. I remember a San Francisco paper that had this great quote. They called us, I don't remember the exact word, but it was real sexy and it dealt with love between these two guys without homosexual overtones. It was the first time you got to see that. It was the first time that two guys got to look at each other with "Nights in White Satin" in the background, no dialogue and them just looking at each other, with no homosexual bullshit. That's a testament to David Burke, Eric Blakeney, Steven Cannell, Steve Kronish, because they wrote the material. Really, all I had to do was act it. I would love to be able to say I deserve all the credit, but that's not true. It was all on paper for me.

Every week I would come down to LA and would battle with these guys about structure, about what we should be talking about, but I would never write dialogue. I would say, "We should be talking about love, and not about bullets." And they would get that. Kenny and I would fight for different things in Vancouver, but it was never really a fight. It was something that they always understood to be real.

"A Deal's a Deal" was sup-posed to show Ray kicking the dog, and I have the knack of kicking the dog and making you feel sorry for me. That's what acting is all about. That's just a little trick that I do, although it's not really a trick. It's something that you're trained to do. I was constantly getting that, but, listen, there was nothing they could do to get me to perform it a different way. It's not that I was stubborn, but that's just the way it was happening existentially. Hindsight, everybody's a genius. While we were doing it, everybody was just doing the best they could. We shot an alternate ending, and I think it was to placate Kenny and I as our swan song together. When we did the episode, Kenny and I were always getting all this fan mail, and we were saying, "The audience wants to see Vinnie and Sonny have a good time. That's what they want, so we now have the opportunity to do it." "A Deal's A Deal" was a whole new episode, so we figured we could do Sonny and Vinnie on the road. They pick up a girl hitchhiking, and they both fall for her, and it's guy stuff. Let's get out of the gangster mode and do a friendship episode, and they were like, "No, no, no, no." They really wanted this episode to make Sonny look bad, and it didn't work. What happened, though, is they gave Kenny and I a little crumb, which was that they allowed us to shoot a tag...we shot two tags. One that was in the show that you saw, and the other tag was Kenny and I in an empty ballroom at night with two girls we had been up all night with. We were partying and having a good time. The camera would start at the end of the ballroom and eventually end up real close on us. We would laugh, we'd do bumps and grinds with the girls and we'd slow dance with them. And there was one guy up there playing the saxophone and that was it. Kenny and I would look at each other and then at each other's girls, and he would get a feel, like kids, and we'd laugh at each other. He was with a black girl and I was with a white girl

who was like a real show broad. It was really the essence of who these two guys are. We'd look at each other, give each other the high sign and start making out with the girls, and then he walked away with his girl and said, "I'll see you, Sonny." It was like real schoolboy stuff. I think it was a little too risque for the guys in LA, and I really think it was to placate Kenny and I.

I warned them. I said, "Don't you get it by now? Nobody is ever going to dislike me. We're eight hours into this show already and it hasn't happened yet. Do you really think it's going to happen in one hour? Let's go in the other direction and make it soppy." They said, "But Sonny is a murderer. He's about to kill Patrice." I said, "I'm doing it, because he deserves it. They're going to love me killing him." "No, no, no." Well, sure as shit....

It did have twinges of *The Idolmaker*. I think David Burke went and took some ideas from it. I remember saying to him that there were a lot of similarities, so what they did was add a subplot about my brother, and my feeling badly about him with the rifle. So, again, I wouldn't let them paint me into a corner. As long as you've got that emotional stuff going, you're alright. And I think that in doing all of this, they've really found a new way of making old shows on television. If you go back and look at *Playhouse 90*, *Ben Casey*, and the early detective shows, they're really about people. What we did in the 70s was put in a lot of action, and I think if you're looking at the top ten shows in television today, you'll see that they're people shows. If you write good dialogue and you have good actors, say it, then all you have to do is be on a nice closeup and you can get through an hour or half hour. We've explored that area in the action crime drama genre, whereas it hadn't been explored since the late fifties and early sixties. **Wiseguy** is an attempt to bring that back to television. I know for me it is. My new series, that's what

Eric and I would like to do and nothing less than that.

I've got to tell you, a lot of what you saw in my performance really was Ken Wahl being so in love with Sonny, and he and I being such good friends, that he really would give me these little directions. Sonny had most of the dialogue, so Kenny was a listener when he was with me. If he had the time to listen he also had the time to see my performance and I would let him direct me. He would, and I trusted him. He'd say, "That take was better, I think you should do it that way," and he'd give me these little things. He'd say, "This isn't real, Ray." Sometimes he wasn't in a scene and he would do that. He was really great, and he was really giving. I knew when I left Vancouver that I had left a little piece of myself with him and vice versa, and it was good that that happened. We probably could have gone on for a few more episodes, but I don't think so.

Once they killed me, it was over. In other words, after the fourth or fifth episode, Kenny and I came down to Stephen Cannell's office and said, "Listen, we think we've got something. I'd like to stay on for a little while." And Stephen said, "I have script commitments, sets are being built and I've got to bring in this new arc." He was very nice to Kenny and I, came up to Vancouver one more time, took us out to lunch and explained to us how he would like to, but he couldn't take that risk then. From that moment on, I was gone; I knew I was a goner and just moved accordingly.

I was getting so much mail, that I had to let people see Sonny again, only as an actor I couldn't come back from the dead. Kenny Wahl had a story that worked out perfectly for him at both levels. For me, it was just about going up to Vancouver and having a good time doing the last episode before everybody broke for Christmas, and it was a reunion. That's really, for me, what it was all about, and for Kenny I think it was the same

thing. I don't want to take a shot at it in any other direction.

You know, Ken Wahl's whole line in the entire show, the one that made me fall in love with him as an actor, was when he said, "This is about the law, man!" For one moment Sonny believed it. At that moment Sonny looked at him and knew it was over; like all the great heroes throughout history he was just waiting to die. That's the whole deal! That's all David Burke, and suddenly Sonny is talking like Abbie Hoffman, and getting away with it.

Another thing that allowed me to know Sonny even better, was for the first time he talked about his old man, and they talked about their fathers. I remember when we were acting it out, I was like choking. I didn't want to cry, so I was choking, holding it in, but, whew, it was real heavy. "Last time I saw my old man he went to buy a cigar." He's standing there telling Vinnie that even though his father had a bread truck and a route, there really was no difference between both their fathers. It was *so* poignant. When I hear "Good Lovin'" I can't help but think of that scene; I sing it in my head. I remember we worked for weeks and weeks, David and I, trying to pick out a song. I remember the last one we found was "Five to one, one to five, no one here gets out alive." I wanted to sing that, or a Doors song, something that had to do with really deep dark stuff, and David wanted "Good Lovin'." I remember we argued about this for weeks, but then the one line made so much sense to me. Sonny was singing into the mirror, "I asked my family doctor just what I had....I said, Doctor, Mr. MD, can you tell me, what's ailin' me?" I said, "Of course, that's the song. How stupid that I didn't see it." That was an interesting thing that happened.

Remember "The Marriage of Heaven and Hell" and the speech that Sonny had made when he was walking around the table? Eric Blakeney had a whole other speech written. About a week be-

fore we shot the show, there was something wrong with that speech; something that wasn't right. What happened was Eric came up to Vancouver with his wife and little baby. I went up to his room to visit him, and I remember being so caught up in the fact that he had this little baby. I grabbed the baby, picked it up out of the crib and smelled its head, and we started talking about life, and that that was what life really was. The smell of that baby's head and how it's interesting that old people's heads and babies' heads smell alike, so the closer you get to the void, maybe that's the scent that emanates from your body. We got into this whole discussion about life and the meaning of it. Whatever I was telling Eric, the next day he wrote to a monologue, so that monologue was really a discussion he and I were having about his baby's head. That's what it was like; that's the artistic sense of freedom you got on the set that day.

It was a great part and read like an old 30s gangster movie, and I knew it was important for me as an actor, not necessarily for my career. I didn't foresee that or think it was going to be great. I just thought it was a great opportunity for me to act. Part of the reason people fell in love with Sonny is that I played him at a time in my life when I had no choices left as Ray but to be honest in my life and in my work and it was new for me then. I had just gotten out of the hospital and been through an ordeal in my life, and this was fresh, new and honest. I had to find the honesty in every line, and I had to play it real and truthful, so what happened is that a lot of who I was seeped into that part. My values, morally, politically, ethically, socially, and it transcended just being Sonny Steelgrave, it became this wonderful guy. It happened because I was at a point in my life where I had no more defenses; all the veils had been lifted from me, and all the walls were torn down.

DENNIS LIPSCOMB

Over the past several years, Dennis Lipscomb has become one of the most in-demand character actors working in Hollywood. His credits range from such motion pictures as Amazing Grace and Chuck, A Soldier's Story *and* Sister-Sister *to* Retribution, *and include such television efforts as* Moonlighting, Call to Glory, Perry Mason, The Day After, In the Heat of the Night *and* **Wiseguy**, *on which he had the recurring role of Sid Royce, "Pat the Cat" Patrice's spy within the Sonny Steelgrave organization. A role he reprises during the series' third season. Most recently, he has had a recurring role on* The Famous Teddy Z *as Harlan Keyvo, the most sociopathic actor ever to come down the pike, a role that is thrilling Lipscomb more than any other he has taken on.*

They're bringing Syd back, which I don't understand. I assume it has something to do with the Witness Protection Program.

I was carted off to jail after Sonny was killed. I have to watch my six episodes to get that whole speech pattern, with all the "Hmm hmm, uh-huhs" and that kind of thing down again. In the first script was this "yes, yes; uh-huh, uh-huh," this whole tick that the character had. When I auditioned for Stephen, that was in the script. I thought it was nice and I did it that way. Then they wrote the first two scripts and it wasn't in there anymore. I said, "You can't drop it on me now, it's part of the character." So I used to go in and put it in places where I thought it would work. I just thought that was a brilliant thing that they gave me.

I've gotten an awful lot of compliments about that role, but I really didn't do anything. I mean, I had two scenes per show, but people for some reason remember it, which is why they're bringing me back.

(I really don't want to do a series.) I quit *In the Heat of the Night.* Fred Silverman tried to keep me on there by saying, "I know you don't want to do a series, but do one....do two, because it's a two-parter," and then he made an offer of incredible money for a regular role, but I wasn't interested. Harlan Keyvo on *Teddy Z*, though, is a different story. This is the kind of character on a TV series I've spent the last eight years waiting for, and this one I'll do as many times as they want. He is just *such* a character, and it gives you a chance to really act. You just don't do a Southern accent and play the mayor like *In the Heat of the Night*, or say "Uh-huh, yes, yes," like in **Wiseguy** and get two scenes per show. I just love the character. You can throw chairs through the windows and it'll work. He's more interesting than most of the pilots I'm offered, where they want me to play the guy who sends out the two kids to solve the crime, or I'm playing the chief of detectives. I read twenty of those a year and

find them to be boring. But someone like Harlan Keyvo...my God!

I've never wanted to be a movie star, honest to God. I just wanted to be a good actor. Olivier is my God. Which is why I won't do series. I told my father what they offered me to continue on *In the Heat of the Night*, and he said, "Are you nuts?" I said, "No, this may not make a lot of sense to you, but I don't want to play the same character all the time." If I had two kids going to college, it might be a different story. I don't have a family, so I have the luxury of being able to pick and choose. I've got my house, I've got my convertible and that's all I need, which is great because it gives me the luxury to be able to say, "No, give me something different." That's always what I've loved about acting. That's why I did thirty three productions of Shakespeare. When I was younger it was a little bit more challenging than the husband in *Barefoot in the Park*. It's really acting. God knows it's not the money anymore, it's the part. You wouldn't believe what I've turned down [laughs]. If I was to do the same role for four or five years I would be a millionaire, but artistically and emotionally I would die. I hope to God my attitude remains the same.

I loved playing that guy (on *Moonlighting*), and it's about as sick as you can get. Once I realized that that guy *never* raises his voice, the rest of it just clicked into place. That's what I love. Give me something that you don't think I would do.

Retribution was incredibly strange with the director, Guy Magar. I had played a bad guy on an episode of *The Powers of Matthew Star*, and that's how I met him. I've played a lot of crazed killers on episodic, because that's what they need every week. The good guys are the running parts. Anyway, I did that show for him, he wrote *Retribution* for me and I said, "Guy, this is totally opposite of what I did for you. How do you know I can do this?" He said, "I just know." He could have gotten that thing made three years earlier if he had cast Keir Dullea, or somebody with a name, but he wanted me for the role. For me, it was a great part, because I got to do everything. It was Dr. Jekyll and Mr. Hyde, which was wonderful. The first movie I ever did was *Union City*, and that was another situation where the guy had written it specifically for me. More friends like that in the business we need. You've got to know what to turn down. I could do a scumbag a week on episodic, but I just don't do it. It's good to have the choice.

I auditioned for Stephen and the powers that be (at **Wiseguy**) and I got the part. I knew I was going to be done after six episodes so I did it, because if he had said this is a running part, I would have run away. I thought it was great, because I was doing six episodes I had time to develop the character and there was a lot of money involved, which was also great. The best thing about it is that all of my scenes were with Sharkey.

I had this scene with Ray, and I was doing the guy from *Moonlighting*. There was a director there and all he had to do was tell me I was doing the character wrong, but I got home and said, "We have to reshoot this." I did something that Sid never did after that, which was to get real powerful. He doesn't have the power. The thing with him is that it has to be like, "Yes, I'd like to have a ham and cheese sandwich for lunch," whereas I was doing the guy from *Moonlighting* where my attitude was like, "I'll cut your throat and feed it to you," which was totally wrong. I didn't know it because it worked while we were playing the scene. It was wrong for the character, and why the director didn't tell me that I'll never know. Why I didn't know, I'll never know, but it's hard to be objective about yourself. Anyway, we reshot it, and from then on I had it clear: "It's just business, you don't have to raise your voice," but not in the sense of *Moonlighting*. I don't raise my voice because it's just business, what are you getting so excited about? It used to drive Sonny Steelgrave crazy. I think the scene that sticks out in my mind the most is when I'm under the table throwing up as he's killing my boss, thinking that I'm next. I was praying that they would leave that throwing up in, and I'm glad that they did. It was wonderful.

This was Stephen's baby and this was the beginning of it, so it would make sense that that was one of the best arcs. It's because of Ray. I thought he was just wonderful.

I enjoyed it. Talk about a great job. I did all my scenes in two days, and flew back for a week. I was getting paid by the episode not by the hour, so it was wonderful. Bless the people that scheduled it, because they obviously did it on purpose. That whole organization is very considerate.

You know, I got in a lot of trouble when I first got out here. After thirty three productions of Shakespeare I said, "Look, if I can do *Hamlet*, I can do *Little House on the Prairie*. Trust me." I couldn't get arrested in New York. I was a classical actor, and that's why I came out here. I had this conversation with the head of Lorimar. She said, "What do you think about acting?" I said, "I'll give you an example. I think Robert Redford does Robert Redford better than anybody in the world will ever do Robert Redford, and it has nothing to do with acting." She said, "You could be in a lot of trouble out here," and I said, "Not if I'm good!" I can't believe I had the balls to say that, because it was the first month I was here.

49

SEASON ONE
MEL PROFITT

Arc Two: Mel and Susan Proffit (Kevin Spacey and Joan Severance)

Perhaps the biggest problem facing the production staff was somehow managing to top themselves, although they never really looked at it that way.

"We never try to outdo ourselves," says Les Sheldon. "We never wonder how we can top ourselves, because we'll just get in our own way. We have gotten into a comfortable level of working as hard as we can with as much ability as each one of us can bring to the show, and we will continue to do that."

Still, there was some understandable concern about continuing the series.

Stephen Kronish notes that, "The relationship between Ken and Ray was so comfortable and the show was working so well, that there were a lot of people saying, 'Well, why are we getting rid of this thing? This is going so great.' But we felt that if we didn't do that, then what is Vinnie Terranova? He's not doing his job."

Eric Blakeney has his own personal opinion on what happened to the series once Sharkey left. "I thought after Sonny Steelgrave, the series lost its edge and never got it back when we went into the Mel and Susan Profitt arc," he says. "I just felt that this was like writing for cartoons. These weren't people. These were psychological symptoms that had nothing to do with human beings whatsoever. We were putting on a freak show from that point on. I myself was never turned on by helicopters landing on boats, James Bond cars and lunatic-psycho killers. They had nothing to do with people as far as I'm concerned. Everybody knows that the first arc was the best and there was no way to get it back, except to cast superstars, rock and rollers, Jerry Lewis, and so on. That's the only way they can get the P.R. and attention, by casting the flavor of the month. Someday you'll probably see Madonna and Michael Jackson as the arch villains."

It's suggested that to his way of thinking, the show took on a tone that was similar to what happened with the James Bond films after Sean Connery left.

"The perfect analogy," he declares. "You have to use sensationalism to sustain the series. Connery had the magic of the personality and the emotion. The series just doesn't have the emotion intact, because Vinnie's not really forming those kinds of complex emotional relationships. His bad guys are clear cut to him. To me, the great thing about the series was the conflict he had in not being able to tell the difference between the good guys and the bad guys. You go undercover with a Mel and Susan Profitt, you know who the hell the bad guys are. Here's a guy who talks to his toes while his incestuous sister is putting needles under his toe nails. They're ordering everybody on the face of the planet killed, and they make fifty million dollars a day with their drug empire. *A day*! There are many countries that don't make fifty million dollars a day. The whole thing was just completely fantastic and far-fetched."

David Burke differs. "There was a very strong reaction to the Steelgrave arc, because this was new television," he says. "It was the cutting edge, and people were saying it was revolutionary and that whatever we did, we'd never be able to do it again. From our point of view, that's invalid. Why would we suddenly lose the ability to do what we were doing? I think what had made the Steelgrave arc unique is that it was simply something we had never seen before. I think we've done much better shows since then, but television hadn't done what we had done before, and that's what made the challenge, 'What's next for Vinnie? What is the natural growth of this character?' It may not be as exciting, but if it's real, that's what's important. Creatively, we're the same people as we were in the Steelgrave arc. It wasn't something that we worried about."

Director Robert Iscove observes, "No one quite knew where to go after Sharkey. He had become such an incredibly strong presence and everyone was saying in the reviews at that time that the show was so much Steelgrave, that they were worried if you pulled him out of this, what do you have left of **Wiseguy**? Kenny proved everybody wrong."

"Independent Operator"

Original Air Date 1/4/88

Written by Stephen J. Cannell

Directed by Aaron Lipstadt

Guest Starring: William Russ, Joan Severance, Clyde Kusatsu, Will Zahrn and Terry Bozeman

In an attempt to ease Vinnie back onto duty, Frank gives him the assignment of investigating one Roger Loccoco, who's either a contract killer or the Angel of Death. "Either way," says Frank, "everywhere he goes, the coroner is working overtime."

Pretending to be an arms dealer looking to purchase weapons, Vinnie hooks up with Loccoco, who takes a tentative liking to him. His cover as Sonny Steelgrave's right hand holds strong, and it's enough to keep Roger interested, although as he notes later in the arc, "Steelgrave's business was so small that my employer wouldn't stop to pick it up. It would have *cost* him money." Ultimately this leads to Roger offering to get him some freelance work, and if it works out he'll introduce him to his employer, Mel Profitt. In the meantime, Vinnie is "introduced" to Roger's souped up automobile, a car that makes James Bond's Aston Martin look like a tinker toy, and the pair go on an assignment to get someone that Mel needs to question. Roger doesn't fill Vinnie in on all the details. It erupts into an exciting car chase which Roger effectively ends by unleashing his vehicle's weapons, obliterating all pursuit, but he's wounded in the process, and knocked unconscious in the resulting car crash.

Three days later he awakens in the hospital, and is told that Vinnie "whacked" the guy they were after. Roger is distraught, stating that they were supposed to question him, but Vinnie offers no apologies, stating that it would be helpful if Roger would tell him these things.

A seed of doubt remains in Roger's mind, and he says he wants to see the body, so he can "count the maggots." Vinnie takes him to the burial site, but nearly gets a bullet in the head for his troubles when he tells Roger the face has been burned off the victim's head. The only saving grace is a medal their target always wore. This is enough proof.

By episode's end, Roger takes Vinnie aboard the Hotei, the Profitt's 200 foot yacht, where he encounters the beautiful Susan Profitt, who chastises Roger for his tendency to bring home "strays." Still, she sees some hope in Vinnie, but they'll just have to wait and see what happens.

"For me," explains David Burke, "the most exciting thing about the episode is we were able to get William Russ to play Roger Loccoco. We knew the episode was leading to 'Fascination With the Flame,' and it was very important to me that we slide Roger under the Profitts, and have him resurface as the ultimate antagonist who becomes the protagonist at the end of the arc. I think it works. It was important from the beginning because Roger is what Vinnie would be if he went bad. Roger was the perfect guy for Vinnie to look at and say, 'There but for the grace of God goes me. If I let how I perceive my duty blind me to what is right, that's who I could end up being.' We kept on building that relationship between Vinnie and Roger where each smelled something in the other one that's not on the table. Vinnie senses in Roger some commitment to philosophy and some commitment to duty that has nothing to do with making money. It has to do with what he believes is righteous, which is something that's not exactly on the table. And Roger smells in Vinnie an undercover operative at work, but can't put his finger on it yet, which was real fascinating for me. It was real important that these guys came to know each other and respect each other."

Eric Blakeney explains that the teleplay for "Independent Operator," written by Stephen J. Cannell, was a "poorly received script, and I know Steve felt really bad about it. That's when the show really started factionalizing and people started working on different agendas. I feel that we as a staff fell apart at that point. Kenny didn't want Ray to leave the show, and I think we were all kind of disappointed, and we were all very nervous about what we were going to do next. Stephen wanted to go more towards using the book *The Underground Empire*, but legally we couldn't. He decided to create the next arc we were going to do and he brought in 'Independent Operator.' We all felt really rotten about it, because it just looked like a hardware show, with a James Bond car and all that stuff. A lot of people were very nervous and everybody was obviously very intimidated and didn't know how to deal with that problem. Stephen was upset, because he had a vision for it that we just couldn't get behind. Mel Profitt was a caricature, as was Roger Loccoco. They were simply caricatures of villainous archetypes that have been on television since the beginning and have been in the movies forever."

"Fascination For the Flame"

Original Air Date 1/11/89

Written by Stephen J. Cannell

Directed by William Fraker

Guest Starring: William Russ, Joan Severance, Kevin Spacey, Clyde Kusatsu, Franklyn Seales, Willard E. Pugh and Will Zahrn

"Fascination for the Flame" is, without a doubt, a bizarre, though highly effective, episode of **Wiseguy**, delving deeply into the realm of Mel and Susan Profitt and

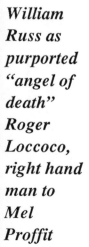

William Russ as purported "angel of death" Roger Loccoco, right hand man to Mel Proffit

giving the audience a taste of what was yet to come. At the outset, we witness Mel's paranoia; his fear that the people who work under him are conspiring to destroy him. Susan makes some security suggestions, and then injects Mel with a drug that allows him to calm down.

The crux of the episode unfolds as the Profitts, along with Roger, Vinnie and other members of security, attend the wedding of business associate and drug kingpin Paco Bazos. Mel actually stops the ceremony, and pulls Paco into another room, stating that he believes his bride-to-be comes from Virginia—Quantico to be exact—and that she is a Federal agent. Paco dismisses this as paranoia, and tells him to get the hell away from his home. He and his entourage do so, and no sooner have they gone than Paco is giving his people orders to kill them all—a fact Frank McPike picks up on his surveillance equipment.

Later, Susan meets Vinnie in a string of suites in the Profitt office building, where they're holding out until the heat from Paco dies down. Vinnie gives her some security details that were missed by Roger. This impresses Susan to the point where she says she senses something different about him, and that intrigues her. They kiss.

That night, Vinnie is called to see Mel in his room for a couple of beers. Confused, he goes and within a matter of minutes, Mel tells Vinnie he had better not hurt his sister, pulls a gun and plays Russian roulette, stating that the idle rich are hard to entertain. He pulls the trigger six times and laughs that there are no bullets. Vinnie then pulls his own weapon, and says, "Let's get something straight. I work for you. You pay me, and I do what you tell me to do. But if you ever, ever point a gun at me again, you're history." He pulls the trigger and a bullet hits the wall, resulting in security breaking in, but Mel dismisses them, stating that he and Vinnie are just playing games.

Next day, Paco calls the Profitts, saying that he and Mel should meet one more time to see if they can salvage what has been an extremely profitable collaboration between them. The two meet, and Mel reiterates that he wants Paco's wife checked out, because he knows she's from Virginia. Then Mel gets a phone call, and he discovers that Paco's people have kidnapped Susan. He is devastated. Paco calmly tells Mel that he wants his drug distribution operation, as well as the personnel to run it. If this happens, in one month he might release Susan, or he may arbitrarily eliminate her. He departs, and Mel starts screaming in fury.

Mel blames Roger for this mishap, and Vinnie, in a desire to save his ass, tells Mel that Roger has come up with a plan to track the food that comes to Paco, as the South Americans have this "thing" for eating freshly killed meat and poultry. The plan ultimately works, and they get Susan back, but in the process, Paco shoots his wife by accident and Roger returns the favor.

Ironically, at episode's end, Mel is hysterical because a newspaper report confirms his fears: Paco's wife was indeed a CIA agent.

"The Profitts were tough to write," says David Burke, "but actually, when you threw all your preconceived notions away and just started to write, they were fun. Cannell created Mel and Susan in 'Fascination For the Flame' and defined them pretty well. They were a psychotic critical mass, and they needed each other to be functional. Mel was raised in institutions from out of the gate, as was his sister. He had a genius capacity, but he was completely sociopathic as a result of being brought up by the bureaucracy, having no family and no love. The only love he did have was with his sister, and they were completely devoid of relationships outside of one another. Anyone outside that relationship was a potential threat, because Mel was crazy.

"He was a great character to write," Burke adds with a laugh, "because you could delve into his craziness as much as you wanted. He was also very self-destructive.

We enjoyed writing Mel—at least I did—and Kevin Spacey never went off the script. Never. And neither did Ray. Actually, actors who stay with our scripts usually give better performances than actors who don't. But Kevin was not afraid of the material, and a lot of actors would have been. He's a consummate actor and he was not afraid to go for broke. He was also getting a lot of 'How are you going to top Sonny Steelgrave? How are you going to top Ray Sharkey's performance?' His attitude was 'I'm not going to worry about it.' He's spectacular. He's an enormous actor and he gave us a great performance and we gave him some very tough stuff to do. I love writing speeches, and I had written a couple of doozies for him that he knocked out of the ballpark. In 'Smokey Mountain Requiem' when Vinnie's quitting, he asks Vinnie, 'What did we do?' And Vinnie says, 'You're drug dealers.' He laughs at him and says, 'That's just a little piece of what we do,' and he brings out this bust of Malthus, pulls the map out of the ceiling and starts explaining his business. Kevin just played it to the hilt and he was great."

He has an equal amount of enthusiasm for actress Joan Severance. "Joan came in to us, and really had not done anything before," explains Burke. "She was so well prepared that she blew us away. The scene they were reading was the scene where she shoots Mel in the toes with his elixir, and you have to sense a certain sensual love she has for her brother. We had fifty or sixty people in there, and they read incest in to it. It was repulsive to them, and they could never get past that repulsion. Joan came in and played it dead on; she was perfect. We sensed a real love for her brother that would manifest itself in almost any form and keep him safe, sound and warm, whether it was sexual or a brother/sister relationship. She was so good, that there was no question in our mind that we wanted her. She did not have enough experience as an actress to be able to prepare as much on an episodic basis as she was on the first episode, so we had to spend a little more time with her in the beginning, but she was a real trooper and really delivered for us. Joan worked hard at it."

"Smokey Mountain Requiem"

Original Air Date 1/18/88

Written by David J. Burke from a story by Jans Tobeason

Directed by Neill Fearnley

Guest Starring: William Russ, Joan Severance, Kevin Spacey, Will Zahrn, Rance Howard, Lou Hancoc, Fred Asparagus and Mark Pillow

Upon recognizing the full scale of the Profitt organization, Vinnie is ready to quit his assignment because he feels it has transcended the jurisdiction of the OCB and is now in CIA territory. The CIA, on the other hand, begs him to stay involved as it'll be tougher for the next person to get that close to the Profitts, but because Vinnie has no authority, he can't agree. Frank actually takes his side, but asks that Vinnie quit "nicely." His response is to say that he'll explain he's homesick, and wants to head back to Brooklyn.

To this end, Vinnie goes to see Roger, who really doesn't want to see him go. In fact, Roger starts hinting at something going on behind the scenes involving Third World nations, but doesn't give any details. It is not enough to whet Vinnie's appetite to stay, and he tells Roger to handle his resignation, but Roger, in turn, says that if he just quits, Mel will extrapolate until he thinks that Vinnie is a cop, then he'll order him killed, and Roger will have no choice but to carry out those orders.

Taking all of this into consideration, Vinnie meets with Mel and that meeting actually concludes in his being given the opportunity to handle Mel's cocaine operation from a small farm in Tennessee. He is told to bring Roger along as *his* assistant. Realizing that this may be an opportunity no other undercover operative may get again, he accepts the supposed promotion.

THE MAKING OF A WISEGUY

Once they arrive on the farm, Vinnie and Roger are told that the farm's owners handle Mel's business because he set up their son and got him arrested for carrying moonshine over the state line. The result was a fixed trial that resulted in a thirty year sentence. Susan told them that if they continued to handle things, their son could probably be out of jail within six years, and they've been cooperating—reluctantly—ever since. When he gets a moment alone, Vinnie uses Federal clout to get their son, Russell Haynes, released.

Overall, the assignment has been a waste, as another druglord in the area has taken control of the trade and left little for Mel. Mel himself shows up near the farm, agreeing with Vinnie that there's nothing left to save. He wants all evidence of his involvement removed—scorched—and he wants Vinnie and Roger back in three days.

Russell Haynes returns home and holds Vinnie and Roger at gunpoint, then brings them to the drug czar, Jesus, and tells him to get out. Jesus refuses, stating that he's still got six years in charge, as was their agreement. A major shootout erupts in which practically everybody dies. Vinnie and Roger escape, refusing to kill the farmer and his wife as Mel had instructed. The OCB and CIA arrive, and confiscate the incredible quantity of drugs on the premises.

Later, Vinnie informs Frank that Profitt's organization is much bigger than anyone had imagined, touching a diversity of illegal interests, so he'll be staying on. In addition, he wants Roger checked out, because the man has convictions which aren't normally found in a contract killer.

"My blemish on **Wiseguy** was 'Smokey Mountain Requiem," admits David Burke. "We had a number of problems with that episode. The second two acts didn't work as well as the first two, but there are moments in it that remain among my favorite. The first two acts are terrific for me as anything I've ever written, where Vinnie goes to Roger and wants to quit, but Roger doesn't want to accept his resignation. He wants to explain why it's important to stay, and Vinnie says there are more important things than money. Roger believes that too, but he can't tell Vinnie what is so important. He talks around it in this bizarre kind of way, talking about holes in the ozone and things like that. Then we went to Mel's speech about Malthus. I had a whole lot of fun writing that stuff."

Eric Blakeney considers this episode and almost laughs aloud. "That was a show where they went off to milk cows, and that's where Kenny just blew up. That was a real disaster for us, and we're talking about having a real unhappy star at that point. He blew up because it was a stupid story. Kenny said, 'What am I doing out here milking cows?' It wasn't just that the story was bad. Kenny is a guy who works very well in an urban environment. After that little fiasco with him down on the farm milking cows, we kind of make a conscious effort to get this guy back to the big city, where he belongs. The rest of the season was just a lot of pushing and shoving and weirdness, and we never really found a rhythm with it. All we could do was grab moments."

Mel Proffit (Kevin Spacey) lives up to his last name

"Player to Be Named Now"

Original Air Date 1/25/88
Written by Stephen Kronish
Directed by Ron Rapiel

Guest Starring: William Russ, Joan Severance, Kevin Spacey, Jon Polito, Jane Brucker and Clyde Kusatsu

In perhaps the most human moment we've seen Mel in yet (and will), he invites Vinnie out in the middle of the night to a local baseball stadium just so that they can hit some balls. Incredible as it may seem, the two actually have a great time, and Mel makes the announcement that he's going to buy a new baseball franchise in Sacramento, and that he's trying to get himself in shape for it.

"Mel," says Vinnie, "just because you own a team, doesn't mean you can play."

"But you're wrong, Vinnie. That's exactly what it means," he replies with a laugh.

Later, Mel is back to his old ways as he starts smashing up their suite out of jealousy over Vinnie and Susan. He doesn't want her to love Vinnie, because then he would be all alone and would disappear.

Once Mel's got his act back together, he and Susan discuss the fact that the team he wants to buy has just been purchased by one Eddie Van Platt, a former business partner of the Profitt's who Mel believes ripped him off for millions. Mel then arranges for Eddie to be on board their yacht that Friday, when a major storm insures that they stay out at sea for a while. That night, he tries to buy the team, but Eddie refuses to sell. Coincidentally, a former lover of Mel's (Jacqueline Devries) shows up, and Eddie is attracted to her. He offers Eddie twenty million for the team, but still he refuses, yet he does seem intrigued by the deal sweetener that Mel offers: Jacqueline.

Eddie has sex with Jacqueline, and comes out of a cabin a little later, stating that the more he thinks about it, the less he wants to sell. It doesn't, he points out, have anything to do with the team, but more that he has something that the other guy wants, and it's a great feeling. Suddenly the kid gloves are off, and Mel starts rattling off various debts Eddie owes whose markers are now being called in. Eddie confidently says the money is no problem, but then Mel lets the other shoe drop: a defense contract that Eddie has upwards of $96 million invested in is going to be severed the next day, a bit of information Mel's sources have been able to dig up. Since Eddie can't get off the yacht and can't put in a call to his broker, he is going to be broke. Swelling with power, Mel says that twenty million is too high for the team. Since he knows that Eddie screwed him on previous business transactions, he decides to pay only six million for the team, and then has Roger lock the man up in the "playroom."

From there, Mel turns his attention to the next order of business: Jacqueline, who he wants Vinnie to throw overboard. Vinnie refuses, and Mel pulls out his gun, threatening to kill him. Vinnie doesn't change his mind, and Mel shoots everything around Vinnie, but not him. Mel decides he's tired and leaves them alone in the room.

At episode's end, Jacqueline goes back to her life without Mel, feeling she'll live a lot longer; Eddie Van Platt is willing to testify against the Profitts after he's put in the witness protection program, and Mel's bid for the team is rejected by a committee of team owners who feel his lifestyle would "cast doubt on the integrity of the game."

Mel sinks into massive depression, wanting the world to be dark forever.

"In 'Player to Be Named Now' we tried to take people like Mel and Susan Profitt and create a connection between them and Vinnie," says Stephen Kronish. "In that episode, Mel wants to buy a baseball team, and it was one of the first times that Vinnie found in this guy that he couldn't connect with, something to connect with. This is a little boy's fantasy. It was also a period in terms of the production and getting everybody enthused again, particularly Ken. There was a scene where they were hitting balls in a stadium. Vancouver has this big domed stadium where they play Canadian football. We were able to get in there one morning to do this scene, and you have to bear in mind that Ken had wanted to be a professional baseball player in his early years. We couldn't get him out of there. He wanted to stay and hit balls all day. That was great, and I think it was also a help in getting a more human side of Mel Profitt."

David Burke adds that, "That was a very hard one for Steve to write because there was no major resolution, no major arrest that took place off screen, but it gave you a sense of the ego of Mel Profitt; how maniacal he was, just to service his own ego. That was real important, to see how this guy played, and how it meant so much for him to own a baseball team. When you're that rich and that powerful, what have you got?"

"Kronish saved the day with that one," enthuses Eric Blakeney, "because Kenny was completely miserable. It wasn't that we had any kind of great story to tell there, but we sat around and said, 'Let's get Kenny in a baseball uniform, put him in a stadium and he'll have a ball.' So Kronish really did save the day. I can't remember a thing about the crime, but Kenny was thrilled. He put on the uniform, started hitting pitches and was happy as a pig in shit. It was keep the star happy time."

"Merchant of Death"

Original Air Date 2/1/88

Written by Carol Mendelsohn

Directed by William Fraker

Guest Starring: William Russ, Joan Severance, Kevin Spacey, Michael Ensign, Paul Verdier, Bill Ontiveros, William Davis, Andrew Rhodes and Nathan Vanering

"Merchant of Death" gives us the true Yin/Yang of Mel Profitt, as he sways back and forth between complacency and unbridled fury at Susan's obvious interest in Vinnie. To this end, he and Susan set Vinnie up as a spy without his knowledge when they go to a party at the French Consulate. There Vinnie is caught in an area he shouldn't be in, and when Susan doesn't vouch for him, he's thrown into jail. The next day Roger bails him out, and Mel eventually apologizes for setting him up, but says that it was necessary because the people who caught him are involved in an arms sale deal to Angola, and Mel has the opportunity to make some fifty million dollars if he can become a part of it. To this end, he arranges a meeting with the Deputy Prime Minister with the intent of purchasing 500 Exocet missiles to be used in foreign nations.

Meanwhile Susan, in an attempt to show Vinnie how she feels, takes him to a motel where they make love, and this eventually complicates things for Vinnie. He thinks he's starting to fall in love with her, even though he knows it's the worst thing he can do.

Later, Mel and Roger go to their meeting. Enroute, Roger suggests that if Mel's immense capital was invested in a sovereign nation, he wouldn't have to buy his way into weapons. The United States would be giving them to him as a gift. "What are you suggesting, Roger, that we take over some third world banana republic?" asks Mel. Roger's only response is, "Wouldn't that be something?", and we can see that the thought is an intriguing one.

They arrive at their alleyway meeting, as do Vinnie and Susan, but moments later a shot is taken at Vinnie. The Deputy Prime Minister then shoots Lizot, the man who had arranged the meeting with Mel in the first place, and flees. Vinnie arrives just as Lizot dies, and is told where important records are hidden—information that will give Mel exactly what he needs to pressure the Prime Minister to cooperate and supply the missiles. Vinnie keeps this information to himself, and Mel's people go around the city looking in potential hiding places. He eventually grabs the material and gives it to Mel, saying that his own people helped in locating it. Mel and Susan leave, with Roger wanting to know just who Vinnie's people are and when he can meet them. This becomes a major sticking point in their relationship.

Frank goes to Washington and puts the pressure on for the missile sale to be nixed, and it seems as though he's successful. Then he and Vinnie are stunned to learn that Mel's sphere of influence is global, and that the missiles were sent to their destination anyway. Now more than ever, Vinnie realizes that Mel has to be taken down.

Says Eric Blakeney, "We were tearing our hair out, trying to think of what to do. We had created this ludicrous character, this kind of Hitler, who made fifty million dollars a day, and we were delving into the outer reaches of weirdness. I don't think we were ever really able to get our teeth into these characters, and David's thoughts on the whole thing was, 'Listen, this stuff is really bizarre. The only way we're going to get our teeth into it is if we just get as weird as we possibly can.' I myself found that weirdness for weirdness sake is a waste of time."

David Burke notes, "In a way, that episode revealed that Vinnie was using the same tools Mel was, even though neither was quite aware of it. Mel managed to get his way and Vinnie discovered it, and in that discovery he understood the depths of Mel's connections and power, and that he was dealing with somebody who is not simply rich and not simply dealing arms, but is dealing with the controls and mechanisms of running government."

"Not For Nothing"

Original Air Date 2/8/88

Written by David J. Burke and Don Kurt

Directed by Bill Corcoran

Guest Starring: William Russ, Joan Severance, Kevin Spacey, Robert Mangiardi, Melanie Chartoff, Joe Shea and David Spielberg

Aldo Baglia, once destined to be a "Prince" of Atlantic City, is avoiding United States officials by hiding out in Vancouver and working in a meat processing plant, as arranged by Mack "No Money" Mahoney. Through a newspaper he's reading in his hotel room, he discovers that Vinnie is working in Vancouver for the Profitts. He calls Mahoney and says he wants permission to kill Terranova because the man betrayed them. Mahoney tells him to forget about it, despite the fact that Vinnie got out of jail on a technicality. Things change, Mack explains, and he should leave everything alone.

"We had everything," Mahoney says, "but that wasn't enough. We wanted more, and now we've got nothin'."

He adds that he's got cancer, and informs Aldo, who hasn't been speaking to his family because the Feds have bugged the phone, that his father has died of a heart attack. Aldo wants revenge, and starts stalking Vinnie.

One night as Mel and his people leave the yacht, Aldo takes aim at Vinnie through his rifle scope. Frank is watching the group as well, but while he's distracted to let

A confrontation between Vinnie and Roger Loccoco (William Russ) in the Mel Proffit Arc

room service in his hotel room, Aldo fires twice, hitting Vinnie in the shoulder and neck. Roger returns fire, but Aldo escapes. Frank comes back to his telescope, and is horrified by the crumpled body of Vinnie.

At the hospital, Frank visits Vinnie briefly, but leaves O.R. almost immediately. Both he and Roger independently come to the conclusion that Vinnie, not Mel, was the *intended* victim of the assassin's attempt. Both want to know why and go about their respective methods of solving the question, with the two closing in on Aldo at roughly the same time. In trying to escape Frank, Aldo makes it to the roof of a building, but Roger arrives seconds later, stating that he knows Aldo tried to kill Vincent Terranova. What he doesn't know is why. Before he can answer, though, Aldo slips on some grease and falls to his death on the pavement below.

Meanwhile, we see more examples of the incestuous relationship between Mel and Susan, his fury over her relationship with Vinnie, her confessing that she really does care for him, Lifeguard closing down the communication center and coming to see Vinnie in the hospital, Mel's also coming to the hospital and using a voodoo crystal to pray over Vinnie's soul, despite his fury, because Vinnie is a mighty warrior who has been nearly taken from them; Roger meeting with Herb Ketcher to get the info on Aldo, and giving us yet another indication that he has a hidden agenda; and Frank, in his best performance to date, being swept into an affair with a local government agent.

David Burke explains that, "There were two important things about that episode. First off, it gave Ken Wahl a chance to rest, because Vinnie literally spent the episode in bed in the hospital. The shooting was perceived to be an attempted assassination on Mel Profitt, which drove Mel crazy and Mel had to find out who tried to shoot him. It also gave us the opportunity to introduce Roger's contact, Herb Ketcher, and Roger goes about the business of discovering that Vinnie was actually the target. It allowed us to turn over the card on Roger that he had his own agenda that had nothing to do with Mel, and he was serving something bigger and more powerful than Mel Profitt."

It's noted that the episode, in bringing back Aldo Baglia and Mack "No Money" Mahoney, provides a significant element of continuity in the series. "It doesn't always work," Burke admits, "but we try to do that where we can. Bringing Aldo back was worthwhile for us. You get to see Roger working as a covert operator, using the tools at hand to deal with the mystery, just trying to find out why Vinnie has been shot. He does sense something in Vinnie and he wants to find out what it is."

"The Squeeze"

Original Air Date 2/15/88

Written by Gina Wendkos

Directed by Bill Corcoran

Guest Starring: William Russ, Joan Severance, Kevin Spacey, Melanie Chartoff, David Spielberg, George O. Petrie, Vito D'Ambrosio, Elsa Raven, Clayton Corzatte, Terry Arrowsmith and Peter Yunker

Herb Ketcher arranges the destruction of S&M Profitt Enterprises by ruining all of Mel's munitions contracts, and thus costing him over a billion dollars. Out of desperation, Mel and Susan come up with the idea of making their drug trade the primary focus of their organization. He asks Vinnie to arrange a meeting with the top don, explaining that he can take out the middle man and get the mob drugs directly from the source, as he has connections that no one else has.

Meanwhile, Herb and Roger meet, and discuss the fact that if Vinnie is successful in arranging a working situation between Profitt and the mob, then their plans will fall apart. Mel will become the most important man in South America, and, as Roger notes, "Why would he want an island when we've given him a continent?"

Vinnie arranges a meeting in New York with don Aiuppo, and he, Mel, Susan and Roger get on a plane for the east coast. Just before boarding, Herb Ketcher informs Roger that Vinnie is an undercover operative from the OCB, and instructs Roger to take him out.

Mel meets with Aiuppo and it seems as though things aren't going to work out, until Mel puts all his cards on the table, saying that he's screwed up his munitions business and that he has let his drug trade collapse. Coming to Aiuppo, he says, is symbolic of coming to his senses. He consolidates the deal by giving Aiuppo a ruin from a 400 year old church that fell during World War II; the church of his father. Aiuppo is genuinely touched by the gesture and Mel's honesty.

In a hotel elevator, Roger is about to kill Vinnie, when he has flashes back to Vietnam, his memories of honor and what he has always believed in. Ultimately he puts his blade away, and walks to his room in silence. In a phone conversation with Herb, Roger is asked if he took care of Terranova, but he replies that he will not kill a brother in arms.

Herb ultimately interferes again, resulting in the drug deal falling apart, thus plunging Mel into a near catatonic state, his mind dancing in and out of sanity.

"'The Squeeze' was there to introduce elements of voodoo and weirdness that I had already written in 'Blood Dance,' which would be the next show to be shot," says Eric Blakeney. "They pulled things out of my script to shove in there and as a matter of fact, 'The Squeeze' was when we had our huge blowout. David rewrote that script, which was written by Gina Wendkos, and I think he exposed Vinnie to Roger Loccoco, which totally undermined my episode that followed it. It was around that time that I left the show."

David Burke recalls that in this episode they had "one scene where Mel goes off to see Roger's people, which we don't see on screen. They appear in 'Blood Dance,' the episode that follows. Mel ends up pretty close to the edge, almost at the end of his emotional rope and that sets up his totally falling apart when he encounters these voodoo practitioners in 'Blood Dance.'

One of the most interesting aspects of the episode is that it introduced actor George O. Petrie as don Aiuppo, a character who would show up once again during season two and play a significant role during the third year of the series.

"When we were looking for an actor to play Don Aiuppo, a number of names came up," says Stephen Kronish, "and I came across George Petrie's picture. I'm a real *Honeymooners* freak—I've probably memorized all thirty nine episodes—and George Petrie was one of the stable of actors that appeared on that show. He probably played ten characters, but was best known, at least to fans, as Freddie Muller, who was the assistant bus dispatcher at the Gotham Bus Company. At that time I think he was doing *Dallas*, although I'd never seen him on it. I thought, 'Jesus Christ, I love this guy,' so he came in and I think he read the scene once. Basically the interview was him telling us Jackie Gleason stories. He got the job and has been one of the best characters we've had."

THE MAKING OF A WISEGUY

"Blood Dance"

Original Air Date 2/22/88
Written by Eric Blakeney
Directed by Kim Manners

Guest Starring: William Russ, Joan Severance, Kevin Spacey, David Spielberg, Richard Portnow, Charlaine Woodard and Mabel King

While Roger has convinced Mel to finance the invasion of Isle Pavot, he has completely lost faith in the proposed ruler, Louis Cabra, who he says is a follower of the dark spirits of voodoo and has put a death curse on him. This concerns Herb Ketcher, who says that if it takes eliminating Profitt, then Roger should, but he wants Cabra in Isle Pavot.

Vinnie communicates with Iemanja, a political opponent of Cabra, who Mel is convinced can help protect him from the dark forces at work. He sees a medium, her aunt, who tells him various things he must do to help remove the curse. Finally, Mel tells Cabra that he will not finance the invasion. He will sell weapons to him, as well as to the other side, but he will not side with a dictator.

Mel awakens in the middle of the night to find that the mystic crystal has disappeared from around his neck, and he cries out that his soul was encased within it. His spirit for living diminishes with each passing moment.

Later, an attempt is made on Iemanja's life, and Vinnie eventually learns that it was the CIA (actually a separate branch of the CIA) who did so. This information he gets from Cabra after pressuring him, and he also learns that many U.S. officials want him to be the president of Isle Pavot, including Roger Loccoco. Vinnie is stunned. Cabra tries to escape, but when he finds a hung goat in his room, he recognizes it as a symbol of death, and leaps out a window.

Elsewhere, Roger has spoken to Herb Ketcher, and as they see their plan falling apart, they realize they're going to have to remove Mel from the equation and see if Susan can be dealt with. Then Roger receives an envelope with the crystal and a note that says, "Mel's Soul." He brings it to Mel, smashes it to pieces with the Malthus bust, turns to Susan and says, "You're free."

Vinnie and Roger both learn that Iemanja has manipulated everyone. She feared for her life, and thus left symbols of death for Cabra that she knew he would take seriously. She is also the one who stole Mel's crystal and mailed it to Roger when her aunt (unbeknownst to them), the medium, put everyone under a hypnotic spell. Turning her attention to Vinnie, she blames him for everything that has happened, as she didn't want to get involved in the first place.

Mel slips into total depression and asks Susan to send him home. Reluctantly she does so, by injecting him with an overdose of elixir, and she casts his body off in a flaming boat, in the tradition of a Viking funeral.

"The voodoo stuff could have played better," David Burke explains. "The first part of that show was very good, because you get to see Mel's paranoia, and he has this conversation with Vinnie where Vinnie says, 'This voodoo stuff is all bullshit,' and Mel says, 'Yeah, it is, but I happen to believe in it.' He's admitted that if he didn't believe in it, it wouldn't matter."

For Eric Blakeney, memories of this episode, his last for the series, are considerably more explosive. "I can tell you that what you saw was not what was on paper," he says. "They made me do nine rewrites of that script and it was the most poorly edited piece of shit I've ever seen. Not to mention the fact that it was supposed to be a love story, but some of the powers that be were not inclined to have Kenny with a black girl. That episode was completely destroyed. It's one of those frustrations because it came out like shit and didn't reflect well for me, although it was probably the best script I'd written for the show. It really had this wonderful

Joan Severance as Susan Proffit

quality of Kenny's guilt as he's once again in a situation where I could put him with someone he thinks is just a regular girl, because he couldn't understand anything about where she was from. In his trying to save her he really created all the horror that came down on everybody. In trying to do the right thing, all this bad shit happened. I really felt that we were on some great territory. We never used any magic in the show, we didn't do anything with the supernatural. It was what these people believed in. If you believe in it, it works. That's what Mel said to Vinnie. It was a lot of fun to do, although I was ripping off a little bit of *Dante's Inferno*. David Burke and I did a massive amount of research on it, and had incredibly accurate stuff in it, but the editing completely destroyed the show. If they would have let me cut the film, I could have saved that piece of shit."

"Phantom Pain"

Original Air Date 3/14/88

Written by Stephen Kronish

Directed by Dennis Dugan

Guest Starring: William Russ, Joan Severance, David Spielberg, Ron Dean, Melanie Chartoff and Ben Halley Jr.

Susan is arrested for the murder of Mel, although Vinnie refuses to believe she did it. She does, however, drop a bombshell: she's pregnant with his child. Roger pulls strings to get her out, and throughout the episode Vinnie comes to grips with the situation, tries to do the right thing by proposing to her and then is stunned to find out from Susan's doctor that she's sterile, and has been for years.

Meanwhile, Herb Ketcher introduces Roger to Henri Lalonde the new proposed president of Isle Pavot. Then Roger is told to obtain cash from the Profitts via Susan and to kill Vinnie. He won't do the latter, although that's not something he tells Ketcher.

He tries to obtain the money in an elaborate plan to convince Susan that Mel is still alive, and that he wants her to give him huge amounts of money. This works, as Roger gets access to over one hundred million dollars.

Roger meets with Herb, tells him about the money, but makes clear that the invasion of Isle Pavot is going to be handled *his* way, or not at all. Ketcher calls his superior, gets approval to follow through with Roger's request, and notes that after Lalonde is president, Roger can be eliminated. Herb eventually runs into a snag in that Lalonde wants seven million dollars to become president as opposed to the agreed upon three and a half.

At episode's end, Susan, who is no longer mentally competent, is taken away to an institution, although she believes she's looking at a house that she and Vinnie are buying.

"In a lot of ways," considers Stephen Kronish, "my favorite I wrote was this one, where we got rid of Susan who goes off the deep end and tells Vinnie she's pregnant with his child. It's actually one of the few scripts I've written where I was so confident the story worked, that the only way I could screw it up would be in the execution of it, which I've certainly done from time to time. I liked the fact that even though this was a woman he didn't love, Vinnie was given a moral dilemma. Even though this is not the woman he wanted to marry, if she's carrying his child, then he has a responsibility to her. He played that beautifully. I will admit that I stole the ending from *A Streetcar Named Desire*, in terms of her going off to look at a house they're supposed to be buying together, when they're actually taking her away. I think it was an effective, emotional show."

"Dirty Little Wars"

Original Air Date 3/21/88
Written by David J. Burke
Directed by Robert Iscove

Guest Starring: William Russ, David Spielberg, Ben Halley Jr., Denis Arndt, Frank Megna, Andy Rhodes, Richard Sargent, Christopher Thomas and Helena Yea

As Vinnie continues his investigation into Isle Pavot, he goes to Roger's loft and tries communicating with his housekeeper, finding out instead that her tongue had been cut out many years earlier. Suddenly a hit man arrives, kills her and tries to take out Vinnie, but is killed instead.

Vinnie waits outside of Roger's loft and sees Herb Ketcher eventually go inside. Arriving at the loft, he sees the two dead bodies, and assumes that the housekeeper and hitman killed each other. He actually starts laughing about the irony of it, and he's still laughing when he walks out of the building to his car. Vinnie tries following him, but Ketcher goes to a small airport and takes off in a private jet.

Vinnie is told to fly to Washington, DC where key officials from the OCB start putting together the pieces, recognize that Herb Ketcher has clearance to the White House, as authorized by Admiral Striken, and realize that they're dealing with an illegal covert operation. Vinnie and Frank take off and go to the area where Roger is. Frank is alone in his room, when he is kidnapped by Roger's people. Roger himself sees Vinnie in a local bar, tells him Frank is fine and that he'll be returned after the team has left. They get into a debate with Roger insisting that he's defending the country. Vinnie wants to know how having his housekeeper killed defended anything, and he goes on to explain everything that happened in his loft, including Herb leaving with a smile on his face. Roger is stunned.

He proceeds to the airport hangar where the group is gathering and gets another shock when he hears Lalonde on the phone with a bottling company that is going to play a major role on Isle Pavot. Herb, not realizing what Roger knows, wants him to kill McPike. He takes him off some distance away and fires a machine gun at him.

Later, he pays off the team of mercenaries and gives Herb an attache case he says contains money. Back at the hangar several hours later, everything seems to be going as planned, until Vinnie and Frank, who was shot with blanks, step out of the shadows. Claiming that Roger blew the mission, Herb attempts to leave, but Federal officers block his passage. Roger is ready to blow him away, but Vinnie interferes, stating that if Ketcher gets off, he promises on his family that he'll kill him. He also points out that in the attache case Herb is holding are photos, aerial maps and the like—all evidence regarding the Isle Pavot invasion.

"You tell me, Herb," sneers Roger, "where it's worth dying for life, liberty and the pursuit of soda pop."

He lashes into him saying all the speeches about making the world safe for democracy meant nothing. It was all about business.

At episode's end, Roger is placed in an OCB safe house, where he talks to Vinnie about his housekeeper, and how much that woman has meant to him throughout his life.

"We begin with just a mop up operation," says David Burke. "Vinnie is not buying into it being over, because he still doesn't know what happened to Roger. Eventually he finds out the truth about the Isle Pavot invasion, and Roger begins to see the truth of what's going on, learning that this invasion is not about freedom. It's about business. Ketcher's been a kind of puppeteer for Roger, and Roger needs to free himself of that. The death of his housekeeper is critical to doing that. The invasion collapses and it sets Roger right, which was real important to us as well. He's not looking to be absolved of his sins, because they're too big and he knows he's committed them, but he thought he was committing them for just reasons and now knows he wasn't. He was blinded and allowed that to happen simply because of his long standing relationship with Ketcher. When Vinnie asks how he's able to justify these dirty little wars, Roger goes on about why he's continuing the battle. It's brought to a halt when Vinnie asks him how he justifies the death of his housekeeper. How did *she* threaten freedom? And Roger has to deal with that."

Director Robert Iscove's memories are a bit more tainted. "Hangar from hell!" he proclaims. "Sitting in the middle of the rain in the middle of the winter in the middle of Vancouver isn't a lot of fun. I did, however think the script was wonderful, and it was great to have a chance to work with that kind of material again after missing the whole Profitt arc. The episode ended with David Spielberg being arrested, and Loccoco is in the safe house, where he tells Vinnie about his housekeeper whose tongue he had to cut out. The one that I did and the next episode, 'Date With An Angel,' was an arc unto itself, and the two of them have been released as a movie in Europe called *Dirty Little Wars*."

"Date With An Angel"

Original Air Date 3/28/88

Written by David J. Burke and Stephen Kronish

Directed by Les Sheldon

Guest Starring: William Russ, David Spielberg, Ben Halley Jr., Stephen Joyce, Robin Gammell, Georgann Johnson, Ray Stricklyn and Tom Hammond

While "Date With An Angel" is a tremendous episode, its summary is a brief one in that this particular story is very linear in nature. Essentially we're watching Iranscam in one hour, as everybody turns against everybody, and almost everyone denies knowledge of a military invasion of Isle Pavot. Herb Ketcher is suddenly a marked man: no one will talk to him. He's at wits end when he meets with Admiral Striken in a restaurant's men's room. Striken delivers a bunch of patriotic claptrap that convinces Herb to protect him when he takes the witness stand.

The rest of the episode is essentially the trial, with all fingers pointing to Herb Ketcher—even Striken's. Roger barely avoids assassination attempts, but he does take the stand. The testimony needed the most is that of Vinnie Terranova—Federal Agent Terranova, and not mobster Terranova. Ultimately he testifies, but from another room where no one can see him, his voice distorted beyond recognition and he is referred to as "John."

The trial comes to an end when Herbert Ketcher, seeing no options left, kills himself.

Roger meets with Vinnie one more time, and gives him access to Mel Profitt's money, in case something should happen to him. And something does, or so we're led to believe, because a boat with him seemingly on it explodes, but one of the final images of the episode is that of Vinnie seeing Roger standing in the streets.

The arc concludes with Vinnie resigning from his position, never wanting to "see another lie" again.

*Mel
Proffit in
a philoso-
phical
pose*

"I felt Les Sheldon did a terrific job on that," states Stephen Kronish. "In fact, some of those characters from that senate hearing on Isle Pavot have come back in the Washington arc of the third season. We like that kind of continuity, because people don't just disappear out of your life. They come back from time to time and we try to do that whenever we can."

David Burke says, "That was some finale for the season. It's really about everybody scrambling to protect their ass, and we meet the guy that Herb Ketcher answered to, Admiral Stiken, who gets off scot free. He manipulates Ketcher magnificently, and Ketcher ends up blowing his brains out. We were very proud of that show."

While the Profitt arc was not as effective as its predecessor, the first year of the series was an overwhelming success.

Eric Blakeney considers the fact that the Profitts and, in particular, Roger Loccoco, have their own legions of fans. "The arc was weird. It was entertaining, but shitty drama," he observes. "There's a certain kind of drama that turns me on, and it needs a certain amount of conflict. Drama for me comes from internal conflicts and making difficult and hard choices. There was no decision for Kenny to make as to whether or not he should bring Mel Profitt down. This sick dog should have been taken out and shot. What's the problem? It's simply a question of is he going to catch the bad guy or not? It's a TV series, you know he's going to catch the bad guy. He has to. If there's no emotional price to pay, then so what? All he's doing, then, is what every cop on TV does every night. He catches the bad guy, no questions asked.

"If you know everything that's going to happen and that your hero is going to defeat evil, big deal," he adds. "I think in many ways movies and television have become like pro-wrestling. It's a cartoon act you know the outcome of, and you're just rooting for your archetype. **Wiseguy** had the chance to break that, and what they really went into was just sensationalistic, sleazy trash, although I know it has a cult following. We had moments in Mel Profitt where we tried to lift it out of the mire of just silliness, and I'm sure it turned some people on. We did get into some entertaining weirdness, but it just had no depth to it. Mel was Blofeld or any other James Bond villain, and that was a major criticism. We went from Ray Sharkey into James Bond land, and it just turned us off. It was realism into fantasy, and I don't think the series ever really recovered."

David Burke's opinion of the Profitt arc is quite different.

"We had a lot of people who showed some strong stuff as actors," he says. "We had William Russ as Roger Loccoco, and Rusty was great. David Spielberg did some of his best work ever as an actor in his role of Herb Ketcher. Just spectacular. Initially, there had been a lot of resistance from all around to doing the Profitt arc, because it was so tough to get a handle on these people. There was also a lot of thinking that these people were insane, they're doing terrible things, so why don't we just take them out in an alley and shoot them? Roger was a linchpin for holding on to that. We settled in to it with 'Player to Be Named Now' and then 'Merchant of Death,' where you began to see the levels at which this guy was performing and how Roger, through his connections with the CIA—although Vinnie didn't know it yet—could put pressure on people in politics, and it became much more interesting for us. It was a very pleasing experience, and when it was all done we looked at the stuff in the last two episodes and remembered the criticisms of getting rid of Ray Sharkey and the question of how you're going to top it. We felt that we had acquited ourselves well."

Kevin Spacey as Mel Proffit

THE MAKING OF A WISEGUY

SEASON TWO
PILGRIMS

Fred Dalton Thompson as Dr. Knox Pooley, leader of the Pilgrims of Promise, in WISEGUY's third story arc

Wiseguy had come off a highly successful—critically and demographically if not in terms of ratings—first season, living up to its promise of pumping new life into the medium. The first season delivered crime drama quite unlike anything that had been seen before.

The critics loved the show. The audience loved the show. It was drawing unbelievable acting talent, and doing its share in turning Ken Wahl and the series' guest stars into media sensations, thus garnering the kind of press attention publicists usually only dream of.

Year two should have been a cinch, yet it seemed circumstances were conspiring against the series, and it was only through the sheer determination of cast and crew that **Wiseguy** held its own.

The first potential disa-

ster facing the series was delivered by the 1988 Writer's Guild strike that virtually brought Hollywood to a stand-still for six months.

"The strike was over during the first week of August," recalls Stephen Kronish, "and we were on the air—having had no scripts or anything—I believe, the last week in September. There were other shows that didn't get on the air until December. We did the full season, which, because of the delay, pushed production back to late April of this past year. Normally you're done early March, so by the time that was over and post production was finished, you were practically in June and it was almost time to go again. There was really no break at all, and I think there won't be until the third season's over. The strike was really costly in terms of screwing up two years worth of lives. We had to jump into it and have had to go on, and that may hurt us more than other shows because of the planning we need to do for the arcs. It's not like we say, 'Let's do *Casablanca* this week, and next week we'll do...' We simply can't do that. We have to sit down and figure out five shows ahead and try to assign those scripts so that all of the writers are writing, and we hope that at roughly the same time we get four scripts in and are able to figure out where we are. But we can't get to writing until those four stories are blocked out, which is very time consuming and, in some ways, the most difficult part of the process. We can't do it on a one episode basis. It has to be planned more carefully, with more of a long-term approach. That's the downside of the arcs."

The upside, though, is obvious to most of the people working on the show. John Schulian, second season story editor who is now a producer on NBC's highly acclaimed *Midnight Caller*, found the arc to be a highly creative form in which to develop characters and ideas.

"Here was a chance to really write and do more than traditional episodic television," he says, "because on **Wiseguy** you take an almost Dickensian approach to television. We run them over 'X' number of episodes, so you get a chance to really write great characters, peel the layers off of them, see that the villains have their charming side and that there's a reason why their underlings or lackeys are attracted to them, and it's a real challenge. This show is probably what *Hill Street Blues* was in its day, which is wonderful for a writer.

Coming on this show, you get a chance to write for wonderful actors. Ken Wahl is probably underappreciated, but he brings a lot to the show and a lot to the actors he works with. And then to have the opportunity to write for the likes of Jerry Lewis, Ron Silver, Tim Curry, Paul Winfield, Glenn Frey and all the rest is really thrilling. You put words on paper and these guys invest it with even more than you may have imagined."

Despite his words of enthusiasm, Schulian agrees with Kronish's assessment of the impact the strike had on the show. "It was kind of like hell for the whole season," he smiles, "because we were constantly up against the gun, trying to get the show on the air."

The first effort of the show's creative team was to bring the saga of Vinnie Terranova back to Earth, so to speak, in order to deal more with the character's background rather than his involvement with megalomaniacs like Mel Profitt.

"The white supremacist arc actually came about the previous May," recalls David Burke. "After a season with characters like Steelgrave and Profitt, where he had to sit back and simply watch and react to them, that Kenny felt as an actor—and for the audience—that it was very important we get to know a little bit more about Vinnie. I thought he was right, and we wanted to do something very simple that was not along the level of what we had done. If we stayed on the track we were going on, going from Steelgrave to Profitt, we would have found ourselves chasing James Bond-type villains."

Ironically, this particular arc began shortly after the incident on the Geraldo Rivera television talk show that involved the racist skin-heads who instigated a riot during the taping of an interview, as well as other highly publicized racially motivated incidents.

"Is life imitating art or is art imitating life?" director Robert Iscove asks rhetorically. "The show does hit some political statement pretty hard, which is all Burke, pushing and pressing. He's really the heart and soul of **Wiseguy**, and he loves making statements."

As far as the show coinciding with reality, Burke himself chalks it off to chance. "Which is kind of funny," he says. "It's nice that it's playing at a time when it tracks with what's going on in reality, but it really was coincidental. That was really strange for us, because we had come up with the idea the previous May."

"Going Home"

Original Air Date: 10/26/88

Written by David J. Burke

Directed by Les Sheldon

Guest Starring: John M. Jackson, Tim Guinee, Marshall Bell, Elsa Raven, Gerald Anthony, Jesse Doran, Jack Orend, Kerry Sandomirsky and Walter Marsh

Picking up almost exactly where season one left off, "Going Home" begins with Vinnie Terranova arriving home in Brooklyn, having quit his position in the OCB. Time passes, and we see that his experiences with Steelgrave, the Profitts and Roger Lococco have taken their toll on him. His hair is long and greasy, he's grown an unmanageable beard and is working in a local garage.

His brother, Father Pete, as well as Frank McPike, express their concern over what Vinnie's doing with his life, but he won't hear any of it. He feels he's given enough, and wants a normal existence. Naturally fate conspires to make this impossible, as the old neighborhood isn't what is used to be. Local businesses are being driven out by foreign investors, racial intolerance is sprouting up and one organization in particular, the Pilgrims of Progress, are gaining a tremendous amount of support from the neighborhood, including Vinnie's young friend, Richie Stamm, who is looking for a direction in his life. He finds it in the organization.

Vinnie nonetheless remains oblivious to it all, until tragedy strikes his family. The Pilgrims of Promise, led by one Calvin Hollis, destroy a synagogue, which Father Pete helps to rebuild. In fact, Pete even goes so far as to be interviewed on television, where he condemns the acts of any individuals who could do such a thing to a house of the lord. Apparently these words don't sit very well with neighborhood people, as Pete is struck and killed by a pick-up truck.

Was it a hit and run accident, or murder? This tragic event is enough to snap Vinnie out of his lethargy. He cleans himself up, shaves his beard, speaks at Pete's funeral and we're left with the definite impression that it will only be a short matter of time before he takes down the Pilgrims.

"The idea of bringing the character back to his neighborhood was Kenny's," explains David Burke, "and it led us to the white supremacist arc, which seemed to be the best infestation of evil we could put into that neighborhood. We were, however, criticized for doing something so simple and something that was without larger than life threats; dealing with rather pathetic characters by comparison to who we had been dealing with, though I thought they had their own pathos. For us to get to know the neighborhood and the roots of Vinnie Terranova was real important, and that arc was the start on that road for us."

Perhaps one of the most shocking moments of the episode was the sudden death of Father Pete Terranova, the elimination of a major character.

"That was actually something that I didn't want to do," says Burke. "There were a lot of arguments about it, and there were too many people in favor it it. In fact, when I caved in to the pressure to kill him, it was on the condition that I could write the episode so I at least had some control over how it happened. I don't think it hurt us, but it lost a character that was close to Vinnie, and he has very few close relationships. That was a tough call to make. Everyone seemed to feel that it was real important to show how, ultimately, the reason for it was right. It seemed very important to us to show how this rather pathetic rag-tag group of bigoted people—people who want to blame other people for their problems and who you kind of dismiss with a laugh—can, if you ignore them, be deadly. That seemed the best way to drive that home. In a way it gave Vinnie the opportunity to think more about what his brother stood for; what his brother's philosophy was, what he fought for. It kind of made more holy for Vinnie what he was trying to do with his life, but in simple terms. I think Gerald did his best work in that episode."

Les Sheldon notes that, "Some of our strongest shows have been freestanders, where we really explore Vinnie as a human being, but 'Going Home' was a gut-wrenching show for me. Not only was I dealing with the white supremacists, but I was dealing with him as a human being, his brother being killed, and it had a lot of strong moments to it."

"School of Hard Knox"

Original Air Date 11/2/88
Written by Stephen Kronish
Directed by Robert Iscove

Guest Starring: Fred Dalton Thompson, John M. Jackson, Tim Guinee, Paul Guilfoyle, Elsa Raven, Marshall Bell, Jack Orend, Kerry Sandomirsky and Meredith Woodward

OCB Director Daryl Elias, who has wanted Vinnie to either return to work or be debriefed, finally gets his wish when Agent Terranova says he will return, but under *his* conditions. He's bright enough to recognize just what he's done for the organization on his first two assignments. First off, he wants a full investigation into his brother's death, believing at a gut level that it was not an accident.

In the meantime, he's having to deal with the confused Richie Stamm, who gets him to attend a Pilgrims of Promise rally in a local hall, where the group's leader, Doctor Knox Pooley, is presiding. Knox stands before the SRO crowd, and delivers a chilling and racially motivated speech that gets everybody to their feet, cheering. Vinnie can't believe what he's witnessing, feeling that Pooley is a con man and everybody is buying into his act. At that moment he decides that Pooley is someone he has to bring down, even though the OCB thinks it's a waste of time.

Vinnie's reputation as a mobster pays off, however, when Calvin Hollis, Knox's first lieutenant, comes to him for weapons. Vinnie is totally condescending and abusive to the man, but agrees to supply what the Pilgrims need—provided that they can pay up front, in cash. Calvin is against that idea, wanting the merchandise first, but Vinnie's physical reaction causes him to change his mind.

Richie, who's finding himself sinking deeper and deeper into the Pilgrims and what they really are, borrows Vinnie's car, and Calvin gets him to be the driver for an armored car hit, where they steal money and kill the security guard (who we eventually learn was actually an off duty New York police officer trying to earn a few extra bucks).

Calvin gives Vinnie the money for the weapons, and it rapidly becomes apparent the Pilgrims of Promise is much bigger than anybody had thought. Ironically, every time Calvin brings up military strategies, Knox changes the subject, concerned more with selling T-shirts, cassette tapes and the like.

Vinnie and Frank work on setting up the deal and it looks like they're going to have the group on conspiracy to commit murder, when Vinnie calls things off at the last moment because Calvin has brought Richie along.

The influence of the Pilgrims begins to expand.

Details Stephen Kronish, "The character of Knox Pooley was played by Fred Dalton Thompson, who was the Republican counsel to the Watergate committee. He's done some acting. We saw him and thought he could bring this sort of huckster thing to us. I don't know that that was our most successful arc, but he was great. I had a good time writing that show more because of one scene, where he's giving a speech to these people and he starts off by saying, 'Who's to blame?' and he goes on from there. I have a feeling that if he had gone to these people and said, 'It's the Jews that are screwing you,' there are some of them that that would appeal to, but there are other people who get turned off to so blatant an accusation. I felt the way I wrote it, and the way he delivered it, was kind of backhanded. Finally he holds up a mirror and says, 'We're the blame. Don't blame the Jews for doing it, blame yourselves for letting them,' which is doing the same thing. I think he was really good, even though he's not a trained actor. He is a

THE MAKING OF A WISEGUY

courtroom attorney, and I guess you could argue that there's not that much difference.

"I must admit," he continues, "that being Jewish, there were a couple of minutes where even as I was writing that speech, that I said, 'Do I want to do this?' I know there are people out there who are going to say, 'Yeah, goddamnit!' That was a risk we ran. I think the network showed some guts in terms of not cutting that or asking us to cut it down. I think the key to any of that stuff, if you look at what eventually became of Knox Pooley, is to let people see these guys for what they are. In a strange way, I think Knox Pooley is one of the most evil guys I've ever written, because he himself didn't believe what he was saying. To me, that's the key. I can excuse a guy who is a pathological anti-Semite or anti-Black, because he truly believes whatever it is he believes, but the guy who knows it's a lie and trades on it anyway to me is far more evil. We tried to set up the kid in the neighborhood as Vinnie's entry into that world. Here's a guy who at the end of that arc said it doesn't matter whether it's ladies underwear, tires or fish, he'll sell it. And he ends up selling condos to Jews in Florida! We certainly did run the risk of being inflammatory about that kind of thing, but had we not done it, it would have been a little false. We needed to say those things to make the characters seem more real."

Says director Robert Iscove, "Working with Fred was great, and the Watergate stories he told were wonderful, but he's not an actor. He's a lawyer, so it was trying to get whatever we could out of him. He went back and looked at all the tapes of TV evangelists, and that kind of thing. His first speech he did incredibly well, just trying to mimic that particular method of speaking.

"And then there was Calvin. As an actor, Paul Guilfoyle comes on the set as the character, and it's a little disturbing being around Calvin all day long," he elaborates. "He's one of the few actors on the show that doesn't just snap into character. It's very strange trying to give him directions when he's reacting and trying to take directions in character. It's called The Method. But he really is a sweet guy. We saw each other in the bar after shooting one night, and he's this nice, sweet, uneffacing human being. Then he comes on the set and does this intimidation number with the other actors, which is what he needed. It took us a couple of days to realize that it was just Paul being Calvin.

"The scary thing for me, however, was doing the Pooley speeches with the extras, because they were all buying it. The speech was so well written that it did make sense from Pooley's point of view. I was saying, 'Wait a minute, we've got to watch out here. We have to be a little careful with what we're saying.' We were telling the extras to respond and cheer and to do a particular thing. You go through the speech to listen to their responses, but they started doing it on their own in all kinds of places. They were cheering, carrying on and screaming for it. That's when you call David Burke and say, 'David, do you know where you're going a couple of episode from now? We've gotta be careful. We've got to make sure that the movement is stupid.'"

David Burke laughs. "Fred is actually a pretty convincing guy, and that's also the danger of that logic. All he's saying is 'You've only got yourselves to blame for your own problems. Get up and do something about it.' You know, feel better about yourself and hurt somebody who's not from your ethnic persuasion. It was such a well constructed speech that it was hard not to see that fifty percent of it made absolute sense, but it's the other fifty percent that perverts logic and reality enough for the bitter man to find satisfaction out of it."

Jonathan Banks looking predictably happy as Frank McPike

77

"Revenge of the Mud People"

Original Air Date 11/9/88
Written by Stephen J. Cannell
Directed by Bill Corcoran

Guest Starring: Fred Dalton Thompson, John M. Jackson, Dwight Koss, Tim Guinee, Paul Guilfoyle, Janet Wright, Jack Orend, James Distefano, William Taylor, Kerry Sandomirsky, J.J. Johnston, Julie Brown and Raimund Stamm

The ramifications of "School of Hard Knox" became apparent here, when Vinnie is arrested (rather violently) for the murder of off duty police officer Emmett Hicks. Apparently the NYPD have made Vinnie's car, and believe he's the murderer. Once taken to jail, the beatings continue, as the cops—only being aware of Vinnie's gangster reputation—avenge their own.

Frank and Daryl eventually use Federal clout to get the battered Vinnie Terranova out of jail, a point which Frank doesn't think is going to do much good as every cop in the city is going to be after him. Vinnie doesn't care, and when he's let out of the car he goes to see Calvin, starts slapping him around and pulls his gun, threatening to blow his brains out for setting him up this way. Calvin pleads for him to calm down, saying that the Pilgrims have even bigger things in the works which Vinnie can make a lot of money from.

Later, Vinnie corners Richie and tries to find out what the hell is going on. Richie is more distraught than ever, not knowing where to turn. He's sinking, and feels that he has no choice but to go forward with the Pilgrims, because if Calvin thinks he's against him, he'll be killed. Believing that he has no choice, Vinnie identifies himself as an undercover cop, and tells Richie that he needs his help to tie the noose around Pooley's neck. Richie argues that Calvin is the guilty party, not Pooley. Vinnie, of course, doesn't want to hear any of it. What he does want is for Richie to keep his eyes and ears open, and report any information he can back to him. Richie agrees.

That night, Vinnie is taken to a remote area where the Pilgrims of Promise have staged a gathering. Knox Pooley, who had previously said to Calvin that he knows the man likes to burn crosses and sing the klan songs, but would prefer that they wait until he's left, addresses the crowd, thanks them for their support and departs, citing pressing engagements elsewhere. Calvin takes center stage, and begins speaking to everyone in a quiet, stuttering voice, but then blossoms to power as his words begin booming to the enraptured crowd.

Meanwhile, the OCB has given Vinnie three letters from a license plate on the vehicle that killed his brother, which were "imprinted" on his body. His search concludes with a green pick-up truck, the twisted metal grating in its front housing a religious medal that Pete had always worn. Vinnie starts retching upon this discovery, and nearly blows his cover.

The next morning, he contacts Frank and tells him that the owner of the vehicle is Stan Corker, and that he's the one who murdered Pete. Surprisingly, he says that he wants the system to take care of this guy, to really drive home the point to all of those people involved. Frank agrees and Stan is arrested, but Vinnie's quest for justice is destroyed when NYPD officers enter Stan's cell, knowing that he was involved in Hicks' murder, and beat him to death. The murder is deemed a suicide, and Vinnie is devastated, feeling that the system has let him down. He puts a phone call into Lifeguard to discuss it.

"That was our most cop-like show," reflects David Burke, "and Stephen Cannell wrote it. There was that wonderful Calvin Hollis scene, however, where he's given his first opportunity to speak, but he can't because he's a stutterer. But when he gets out there, he suddenly becomes Hitler, and the actor who played the part, Paul Guilfoyle, was spectacular. No one said, 'Do Hitler,' but when we got the dailies back, his mannerisms were subtle enough to not be an imitation, but you could see this is where he drew his spirit. He was wonderful."

"Last of the True Believers"

Original Air Date 11/16/88

Written by John Schulian

Directed by Robert Iscove

Guest Starring: Fred Dalton Thompson, John M. Jackson, Ken Jenkins, Tim Guinee, Paul Guilfoyle, Alan Burke, Richard Lawson, Charles Siegel, Dwight McFee, Mark Acheson, Meredith Woodward, Catherine Pope, Bernie Adelberg, Marjorie Morris and Alvin Lee Sanders

In "Last of the True Believers," everything comes to a head, beginning with *The Alexander Hardin Show*, a television talk show ala *Donahue, Geraldo, Morton Downey Jr.* and *Sally Jessy Raphael*, on which Knox Pooley appears with people representing Jews and blacks. Naturally it's only a matter of moments before things become explosive, with Alexander Hardin launching a verbal assault on the Pilgrims of Promise, and then kicking Pooley off the air. Knox goes willingly, but not until his "800" number is flashed on the screen, as the two had previously agreed.

Calvin is infuriated by Hardin's insults, but Knox brushes them off, stating that Hardin's just trying to give his audience a good time. If Calvin wants to talk to him, then he's more than welcome. Unfortunately, Calvin does more than talk as he follows Hardin into the men's room, and bludgeons him to death with a trophy the man had just been awarded by a Jewish society.

Back at their motel room, where Calvin has hidden the trophy so no one could find it, Richie is helping Knox clean things up and tries to talk to him about a cancer that is eating away at the organization, but before he can continue Calvin walks through the door, and instructs Richie to go in the back room and gather up materials that are left in there. He does so, and is horrified to find Hardin's trophy. Panicking, he exits through a back door. Calvin goes into the room, finds that Richie is no longer there and immediately checks under the bed, only to find the trophy gone. Knox demands to know what's going on, and Calvin stutters the answer, detailing the murder of Alexander Hardin. Pooley is furious, screaming that Calvin has ruined everything. People were just *giving* them money hand-over-fist and now he's destroyed a perfectly good business operation. With that, he starts slapping Calvin around and the man, now on his knees and in tears, says, "Please don't hit me daddy."

Knox is appalled. "I ain't your damn daddy. Now get out of here, and don't ever come back!"

Crushed beyond words, Calvin leaves, his sanity now completely gone.

Between all this, Vinnie and Frank have been trying to come up with the evidence they need to arrest Pooley, but haven't had much luck. Then Richie shows up with the trophy and it seems like enough. They proceed to the motel, where Knox claims his innocence.

Meanwhile, Calvin goes to the home of black activist McGill, and holds him hostage. He allows McGill's wife and kid to leave, but when one of his own people questions an order, Calvin shoots him, causing the man to fall on the stove, where his body catches fire. It's only a matter of time before the entire house is in flames, but he sits there, wanting to get Knox Pooley on the phone. Eventually the police arrange it, and he starts going through a speech about how everything he did was for the benefit of the Pilgrims of Promise.

An explosive moment between Vinnie and Pilgrims of Promise lieutenant, Calvin Hollis (Paul Guilfoyle)

Knox couldn't care less. The only thing he wants Calvin to say is whether or not Knox himself had anything to do with the murders that have taken place. Calvin responds in the negative, and it's enough to get Pooley off the hook, much to Vinnie's disappointment. He tells Calvin to seek some help, and gets off the phone. Then he turns his attention to Richie, welcomes him to the real world and delivers a spiel about how he's always been a salesman, and this was just one more thing he had to sell. Richie is crushed, having completely believed in Knox's words.

Back at McGill's house, the man, who has the barrel of a gun taped to his chest, convinces Calvin of the fact that Pooley is a phony and that Calvin is the true power behind the Pilgrims of Promise, and if he gets them out of the house before they burn to death, he'll help the public see that. These words seem to get through to Calvin, but a stumble causes the gun to go off, thus killing McGill. Horrified by this latest atrocity, he moves outside and the police, seeing the gun still taped to his hand, open fire, killing him instantly.

The episode ends with Knox Pooley, the ultimate salesman, living in Florida and selling condominiums to elderly Jewish couples.

Recalls John Schulian, "After we saw the first cut of the episode, the lights went up in the screening room and Stephen Cannell said, 'I've been in this business for twenty years, and that's the single most violent episode I've been associated with.' It's very interesting, because Stephen Cannell has probably killed more people on television than have died in all the wars that have ever been fought. But his violence has always been with a wink and a nudge, and in 'Last of the True Believers' it was random, and it was ugly and it was real. Calvin and his two dummy henchmen burst into the home of McGill, a well spoken, well educated black activist played by a wonderful actor named Richard Lawson. One of the guys says, 'Don't hurt the woman and children,' and Calvin turns around and shoots him. It was just nuts, and then the body caught on fire on the stove and Stephen Cannell sat there watching his whole empire crumble. But it was wonderful, because then the house starts burning down, one guy jumps out a window, and Calvin and McGill are stuck in the house, with a gun taped to McGill's chest, mainly because television won't let you tape it to his head. Then they call up Knox Pooley. Now remember, **Wiseguy** was always accused of having homoerotic themes. The guy from *Vanity Fair* had great fun with Vinnie and Sonny. Anyway, it became plain that Calvin was looking to Knox Pooley as a father figure.

"It was really nuts," he adds, "and I suppose the episode stamped me as a blood-and-guts guy at the show, which is kind of odd since the year before I had been writing *Slap Maxwell*. Then there was that farewell speech, where Knox Pooley has been selling heat, and there's no more market for it in Vinnie's neighborhood. The next time we see him, he's in Florida, selling condos to the very people he was preaching hate against. What was interesting in the last scene, was that Fred Dalton Thompson as Knox Pooley rubs his hands together and does sort of a Groucho Marx thing with his eyebrow. It certainly wasn't the greatest thing I've ever written, but it was fun in a looney kind of way. For a not terribly good arc, I thought it was a good episode."

Explains director Robert Iscove, "The scene inside the house where Calvin shoots the guy, and he falls on the stove and catches fire...there was a lot of talk about gratuitous violence and that we should be censoring ourselves. We were discussing moral dilemmas. To me, if you're going to show a guy who is into white supremacy, you have a moral obligation to show that it leads to gratuitous violence, but how do you show that without doing violence gratuitously? David Burke started referring to me as G.V., after that, which stands for Gratuitous Violence. That whole ending was difficult to do, because when you do fire like that, you can only be in the room for about ten seconds, because the smoke and fumes are too much. So we were doing all those takes in ten second intervals, and waiting twenty minutes between. Also, when Cannell saw it, he actually went through the roof. I suppose he read the script, but didn't realize how horrific it is when it actually translates and leaps off the page at you. It *is* pretty brutal, but the next week on the *Geraldo* show, they had their riots, so it showed that what we were doing is much less (violent) than the reality of what happens in situations like this."

John Schulian points out that there was never any intention to have Knox Pooley killed. "We always wanted the bad guy to get away," he explains. "One of the bad guys died, but we wanted Knox to get away, because I think in a lot of ways that's the way life is. He was a manipulator and was far more evil in the long run than the guy he was using as his tool."

David Burke concurs. "I think that Knox Pooley escaping is probably the most important statement we've ever made," he says. "I think that for me he represents everything that's wrong with the American economy; that there are so many people who see their lives that way. They feel like they don't have a responsibility to the way society functions; that if they're not actually committing a crime, then they're leading a good life. Knox put on a little show for these people, sold his records, tapes and books, stayed in cheap motels and he moved on. It used to be cars and refrigerators, and now it's fear and loathing. At the end, it turned out to be condos in Florida. The fact that he could motivate a small army to do destructive things and walk away unscathed is something we see in our own lives on a daily basis, and we ought to think twice about doing business with those people again."

Surprisingly, the majority of the people involved with **Wiseguy** consider the white supremacist arc to be among the weakest of those presented during the second season.

"It's probably the least entertaining of the arcs for the audience, I would guess, because it's so bleak," comments David Burke.

Director Robert Iscove adds, "It was not my favorite arc. It felt a little unrealized, although it had its points to it. It felt more like a filler arc. Where do you go with it? It never got that crystalized. What was Vinnie's real point of view with all of those people? It got harder to do the show, because he was so involved with Sharkey, and he had this dichotomy in their relationship. Profitt was so crazy that he couldn't relate to him at all, but he did have a relationship with Lacocco, so that there was a give and take about how he was feeling about the job. Then you get to the white supremacist arc, but because the Tim Guinne character wasn't that realized or wasn't an equal to Vinnie, it's very hard to play anything other than these guys are totally stupid and he has to bring them down. The actor playing Richie Stamm did a nice job, although his part was a little undefined. He kept saying, 'Mr. Pooley is really true and really right, and you can't do that.' Well, he never went beyond that with Vinnie. It was very hard to structure what he buys into and what he doesn't buy into, and what the turning point is for him, still believing in the one man even though Calvin is subverting the whole thing. His relationship with Vinnie never really changed, and as a consequence he became this whiny kid. There was no real jeopardy. They wanted to avoid traditional jeopardy on the show, but you never felt as though there was any real threat."

Former Watergate lawyer Fred Dalton Thompson as Knox Pooley

PAUL GUILFOYLE

To hear that Paul Guilfoyle has been deeply involved in a desegregation program for the past twelve years causes a fan of Wiseguy to raise an eyebrow. To them the actor is best known as white supremacist Calvin Hollis in season two's first arc.

Besides his stint on the series, Guilfoyle has appeared on Broadway in "The Basic Training of Pavlo Hummel," "Richard III" and "Glengarry Glen Ross," on film in Wall Street, Beverly Hills Cop II, Three Men and a Baby, The Serpent and the Rainbow *and Robin Williams'* Cadillac Man, *and in such episodic television series as* The Equalizer, Kojak, Miami Vice, Spenser: For Hire, Crime Story *and Stephen Cannell's* UNSUB.

What I enjoyed most about working with this group is that they started out with an idea that they were willing to collaborate on. Everyone involved was very good and pretty open. They opened up the creative window so that everybody could fulfill themselves and the role by participating to the limit that they could. They opened up the idea of how I wanted to pursue this character. They encouraged me to invent and investigate all the aspects I wanted to go with. They never got corporate on me or did anything like that and were really trying to get creative energy into a fast process. Being from the theatre, which is where I come from, I'm used to working from the point of view of character and we got a chance to do that.

Television is so quick that you have to make a decision and go with it, but this felt a little differ-

ent. I'm always interested in exploring the psychological pain of these bad guys so they don't just become the guy in the black hat and the guy in the white hat, even though Vinnie Terranova sometimes wears the black hat, but he is the good guy. Still, it's fairly transparent, you can see who's good and who's bad, and I didn't want to do that with this character because he was so horrible and so much the antithesis of my own personal politics. I'm here in Boston now working on a desegregation program I've been involved with for twelve years. I tell these kids I work with, mostly black inner city kids, Cambodians, Hispanics, that I'm going ahead and doing one of these roles and they should understand this totally from the point of view of an actor working.

I must say that the people who do come up to me and talk about **Wiseguy** in the streets always want to talk about the acting rather than relate me to the character at all, and I feel that's a great accomplishment. Usually people go, "You're the guy who does this and that," but in this case they all seem to know that there's a really good process going on. That's just a tribute to the producers and writers who encourage this creativity, which I think is a great thing. I love the whole idea of creating

psychological quirks for the character, things that would be exhibited as a metaphor for him as well, like a speech impediment. They were open to it and that was very encouraging, especially when it came to Calvin's stuttering. It wasn't like an old gangster movie in the '30s where the guy would say, 'B-b-b-b-butter.' Instead it comes from the breathing, and it's very subjective and comes on and off at different times, and they went along with it. Those are my kudos to the team that work on the show.

In Calvin's mind he wanted to (imitate Hitler), but a big obstacle was who he was as a person. He felt the power of the crowd, and changed. There were some Nazi feelings there, but it was more the spontaneity of the discovery of that fascist power. I did get a whole bunch of books on Nazi Germany and read up on it and came to feel that Calvin was more of a classicist as opposed to just a white supremacist in the new order; guys who are more red necked. He was locked more into the whole Nazi sensibility right down to the way he dressed. I wore clothes that were too small for me, because everything I did was designed to make me feel tighter, more restricted, repressed.

The Calvin I thought had power was the Calvin who could arm himself and go into the woods. When we went on these maneuvers in the woods, and it was real para-military deals. These men would camp out, walk around in their berets and try to act macho. I felt that was a part of his personality, the whole aggressive and violent side. I do think there were a couple of sides to him, and that he could never explain himself or lead a group in speech. He also had these petty problems like jealousy and trying to manipulate this father figure, Knox Pooley. In trying to get love and acceptance, he was always manipulative and weak. Then when he had to exhibit his other tendencies, they

PAUL GUILFOYLE

leaned more towards violence and power, and he was more comfortable. He was less comfortable asking things like "How are you feeling at the moment?" Expressing love or feeling it in any way was all twisted for him. So there *were* two sides to him. I did work on this character in a way, and what I liked about working in Vancouver is that I could say, "No, no, that's not right, this has to be like this, let me do it that way." They pretty much let me do that and then I was able to control the consistency of the character and create the kind of thing you saw, a three dimensional person that had all these complications. In television, most people just want the bad guy to be so bad the good guy has something to go up against. You can see that as well. He's a bad guy, there's no question about it, but you can maybe understand the psychology of his pain and maybe see a human being who is wracked and riddled with problems and disorders. It's not easy for him to deal with what he's feeling. Even in a motel room where he gives somebody a book, it becomes this amazing emotional gesture for him, whereas we would do things a little easier. Nothing was easy for this guy. He was full of conflict and pain, and for an actor that's wonderful to dig into. For some people it may be over the edge, because it's really out there in that risk area.

One scene that I did try to turn was where I hit the guy with the trophy. It was written in the script that he went into the bathroom first, I went in and hit him over the head with his trophy. I said, "I like this guy to do things that are impulsive. I don't think he's that kind of a killing machine." I suggested that I be in the bathroom washing my hands, I see him come in and recognize the opportunity there and hit the guy. So we did it that way, and then when I hit him the actor laid across the floor, I played this thing where I couldn't step over him. I got totally frightened. I wasn't so much interested in the act of violence it-

self, but what happens to a guy like that who decides to do it, the guy falls in front of him and then I had this complete child-like tantrum breakdown where I couldn't move. He wasn't a real hard assed killer who's professional and good. This is a guy who saw the opportunity, did it and then afterwards was in a complete crazy mode. I felt that that broke him, which led to him confessing to Fred and from then on he was lost; he went over the edge. So that scene where I became a little boy, that was all the stuff that was slightly held in and repressed. This need for a fatherly love started to come out. I must admit that they wrote it pretty pointedly. I didn't think it needed to be written as hard, but it came across pretty strong. I always loved that scene the best, though, because Calvin cracked up right there, and it manifested itself in a way that he was trapped in the bathroom. He was paralyzed. This person was mixed up, but I enjoyed getting this guy out there. He wasn't just a second henchman to the character that I thought was a complicated, interesting role that Fred played.

He realizes that there's nothing in his life other than working and contemplating and thinking about how to manipulate this group. One time Fred and I got to talking, and we thought we were going to get killed from both sides. Anybody who was liberal and had a reasonable, political sense would think we were just being a—holes for saying this stuff. Also, the people from the New Order were going to think we were jerks as well. We thought we'd get hit by everybody.

We were filming when Geraldo's thing happened. It was so close together, and at that point I realized how prevalent it was. Maybe we are speaking to a certain segment of this community. Remember, my politics are all about desegregation. For the last twelve years I've helped kids form a group that meets every day and works on writing and playwriting. This is my neighborhood where I

grew up in South Boston, and racism was a very major issue here. I've been working on the other side of the issue so long, that it was interesting for me to do **Wiseguy**. My feeling is that if you're raising the issue at all about racial problems, then it is politically correct. It seemed like a good issue for Vinnie Terranova to get involved in, and I always liked the idea that he was reluctant to get back into his thing at the beginning.

I'm not always aware of how I work, but I do have a way of creating a lot of privacy and keeping my world free of outside influences. I'm very social. I love hanging out with everybody and I had a great time at the Christmas party, but during the day I tried to keep my mind set on Calvin. Some of the stuff required from me in that was, emotionally, very full, even though it was necessary to create that kind of character. But I would stay in character a lot. The one thing I'd like to add is that this whole notion of collaboration was really something that was very impressive to me, especially within the confines of television. Also, because they have arcs and look at things over a period of episodes, that focused the shows on character, behavior, intricacies and developing those characters. I was actually kind of sad that they weren't doing eight of them or something, because I feel that after you get into a few, you could develop someone's world a little further and a little more realistically. I think everyone was capable of that and everyone believed in that, and that was the greatest thing as an actor to have that kind of support, and the opportunity to watch character behavior as a way of expressing, rather than just lines and a storyline that make you understand a character. People who watch over and over get to know and expect the characters to do certain things, just like the way we look at our friends and our world as we notice people's behavior and how they express themselves. We know what they say isn't necessarily how they feel, and that was the great thing they were working on.

Overall it was a wonderful experience, and it was really a thrill for me as an actor to have been involved with the show.

BROADWAY
THE BASIC TRAINING OF PAVLO HUMMEL
 RICHARD III GLENGARRY GLEN ROSS

OFF BROADWAY
 MINK ON A GOLD HOOK
 T.H.E. VAMPIRES
 HENRY V
 IT'S ONLY A PLAY
 LOOSE ENDS

REGIONAL
 THE DOWNSIDE
 GORILLA
 HOT LINE
 RICHARD II
 MUCH ADO ABOUT NOTHING
 AMERICAN BUFFALO
 DEATH OF A SALESMAN
 MAN AND SUPERMAN
 CURSE OF THE STARVING CLASS
 BLOOD WEDDING
 MEDAL OF HONOR RAG
 CAT ON A HOT TIN ROOF

FILM
 CADILLAC MAN
 DEALERS
 SERPENT AND THE RAINBOW
 WALL STREET
 THREE MEN AND A BABY
 BEVERLY HILLS COP II
 HOWARD THE DUCK
 THE LOCALSTIGMATIC

TELEVISION
 KOJAK
 THE EQUALIZER
 A MAN CALLED HAWK
 MIAMI VICE
 BIG TIME
 UNSUB
 WISEGUY
 INTERNAL AFFAIRS
 SPENSER: FOR HIRE
 CRIME STORY
 KATE AND ALLIE
 LAW AND *ORDER*

Season Two
DON AIUPPO

"Aria For Don Aiuppo"

Original Air Date 12/7/89

Written by Alfonse Ruggerio Jr.

Directed by Jan Eliasberg

Guest Starring: Ken Jenkins, Swight Koss, Elsa Raven, Kerry Sandomirsky, George Petrie, John Destrey, Karen Kandazian, Paula Shaw, Tony Romano and James Costy

The plot for "Aria For Don Aiuppo" is a simple one: Aiuppo, who we met during the Mel Profitt arc ("The Squeeze"), meets Carlotta Terranova at a church function, and the two of them, who had once been very attracted to each other, have some of their feelings rekindled. However, she won't have anything to do with him because of "the business," but he swears that is all behind him now. Eventually she lets her guard down, and the two of them start falling in love.

Vinnie's problems, however, are just beginning, as the OCB frowns on the entire relationship. It simply doesn't look good for the mother of one of their key undercover operatives to be involved with a mafia don. To this end they do some searching, and discover that he never became a legal citizen, and arrange to have him deported. Vinnie is furious, feeling that his mother's happiness is at stake. He and Frank ultimately go along with a plan in which Aiuppo and his brother change identities, with Tito, who wants to return to his birthland, being deported to Italy in his place.

Aiuppo and Carlotta embark on their new lives together, with Vinnie being given his mother's house.

"I love that show," enthuses David Burke. "To have Vinnie's mother marry an Italian don was an outrageous conception in a lot of ways, but it worked so well for me. The ending of the show was not accomplished quite right—it read better than it played in terms of the switch with the brother—but that Vinnie has to deal with the fact that his mom's in love with somebody and it's getting him in trouble is interesting. It's still his mother and he finds himself confronting Aiuppo, who's attitude is, 'I'm in my garden, what are you bothering me for?' A great show, and one that worked for us. You also got to see the guys that Frank worked with who were trying to deport the guy, and they say, 'We wish we could help him, if we'd only known about his relationship to Vinnie,' so you get to see the human side of the bureaucracy too, which was really nice."

Vinnie dances with his mother at her wedding to former crime boss, Don Aiuppo

THE MAKING OF A WISEGUY

SEASON TWO
RAG TRADE

Ron Silver and Jerry Lewis as David and Eli Sternberg, struggling businessmen in New York's garment district

When the creative team of **Wiseguy** decided to have Vinnie Terranova investigate the garment industry—or rag trade, as it is more popularly known—they scored a major coup when they cast veteran actor Jerry Lewis as garment czar Eli Sternberg, then were able to get Broadway/film star Ron Silver to portray Eli's son, David. This bit of casting added legitimacy to the proceedings, and garnered the show even more respect from the critics.

It seemed as though nothing could go wrong, but as fate would have it, something did. Ken Wahl was seriously injured on the set and would not be able to complete the arc.

"The camera dolly backed up over him not once, but twice," says John Schulian. "He injured his ankle and couldn't walk. He tried, but kept falling down, so it be came painfully apparent that we were not going to have Ken Wahl for the last four episodes of the five episode garment industry arc. We were up against the wall and had two options: shut down or get another actor to replace him. David Burke prevailed upon Tony Denison, who had been in *Crime Story*, and we got him to portray John Henry Raglin, a character created out of necessity and terror. Getting Denison was just a blessing for us, because he's a terrific actor. He went in there under the worst possible circumstances and made it work, despite the fact we really put him through the ringer in an emotional sense. His character, when we first met Raglin, was very remote and gradually we worked our way into who he really was and what particular demons afflicted him. By the end, I think he was really stripped bare."

David Burke details the hiring of Denison from his point of view: "Kenny is the first guy to say it takes all of us to make the show survive. One of the reasons the show works so well is that there's enormous respect for what everyone does on it. We love Ken Wahl and we were so happy to see him back. At the same time, Kenny loves us and doesn't want to see the show without us here. There's a team spirit that is rare in this business, and I think that any show that works well must have a team that plugs into each other very nicely. But Tony did great, and he also came in at a moment's notice. I called him on the set of a movie he was doing and I said one of those things you always wonder how a friend will respond to if you ask him. I said, 'Tony, I need you to get on a plane, go to Vancouver and do four episodes of **Wiseguy**. You'll play a guy named John Henry Raglin and he's taking over Vinnie Terranova's assignment. I can't tell you anything else, because it's not written. Honest to God, Tony, if you don't do this, I'm going to have to shut down my show. And I don't know who else I can pick up the phone and call, who's got the goods to carry the show.' He said, 'Well, okay, I'll do it, David. If you're in that big a crisis, I'm available and I'll do it.' And he did it for me. That meant a whole lot. I think he benefitted from doing the show and I think we gave him great material. It was a big risk on his part, and he came through in spades."

Interestingly, despite its numerous problems, most people consider the rag trade to be one of the best arcs, second perhaps only to Sonny Steelgrave.

"I think the rag trade is *the* best arc," Burke proclaims. "Everybody thinks the Steelgrave arc was spectacular. It was good for us, we were very satisfied with it, and no one had done that on TV before in quite the same way. There's that initial surprise that you get from the Steelgrave arc and the relationship between Vinnie and Sonny, which you will never get again no matter what you do. Even when you better yourself, it's still that initial jolt in seeing something in ways that were new for television, and you can't match that feeling. That's like seeing fireworks for the first time. Later they might be bigger and better, but it's not the same reaction. I think that the garment district was our best work. Maybe I feel that way because Ken got hurt in the first episode, and we had to scramble to make it work and keep the show on the air. And we *did* make it work."

"Seventh Avenue Freeze Out"

Original Air Date 12/14/88

Written by David J. Burke and Stephen Kronish

Directed by Robert Iscove

Guest Starring: Jerry Lewis, Ron Silver, Stanley Tucci, Patricia Charbonneau, John Santucci, Harry Goz, Jack Wohl, Blu Mankuma, Dwight Koss, Pedro Salvin, Pamela Hart, Lorena Fox, Jennifer Griffin and Paul Beckett

We are immediately introduced to the sometimes volatile, never dull, relationship between Eli and David Sternberg, a father/son team running Elrose Fashions in the garment district. Circumstances have resulted in their needing two million dollars for a dress shipment, and finding themselves unable to come up with the cash. They go to local loan shark Johny Coke Bottles but are told he doesn't have that kind of money. There is only one place on 7th Avenue that does: Rick Pinzolo. David is against the idea, knowing that to deal with Pinzolo is to sell your soul to the devil and that he will only be waiting for the right moment to "acquire" Elrose. But Eli will hear nothing of it.

A deal is set, and when David and Pinzolo are alone, we quickly come to understand that the two of them have some kind of history together, but that doesn't change Pinzolo's ruthlessness as he warns David not to get in his way when it comes to business.

Feeling torn in the middle, David goes to the government and pleads his case, stating that he's willing to work with them just to get Pinzolo out and save Elrose. Having always wanted to investigate the rag trade, the job is handed over to the OCB and Frank, in turn, says that he wants to give it to Vinnie. To this end, David and Vinnie meet so that Vinnie can get a feel for the man, and decide whether or not this is an assignment he wants. He ultimately agrees to come on (a fact which Eli is very much against, but David insists and wins), and his first order of business is to put some pressure on Johnny Coke Bottles to find out why he wouldn't loan Eli the needed cash. To this end, he comes into Johnny's office, perhaps a little bit too cocky for his own good, and is struck down by a stun gun. Then Johnny picks up a baseball bat and smashes it down on his leg. Vinnie has to practically crawl out of the office before more serious harm can be done to him.

At home in Brooklyn, nursing his smashed leg, Vinnie is visited by Pinzolo, who is a bit upset that Vinnie began working for Elrose, and never went to see him at all. Vinnie apologizes, trying to get on the mobster's good side, and is given a beeper. Apparently Pinzolo believes that if Vinnie works for Eli, then he works for him, although this is a fact Eli needn't be made aware of. Before their conversation ends, Vinnie asks if he's responsible for his leg, to which Pinzolo responds in the negative, thus opening up the possibility for revenge on Vinnie's part.

Vinnie's problems intensify in the form of Eli Sternberg, who wants him out of his business. It is only because Vinnie uses Federal clout that he is able to have a ship-load of dresses held up in customs processed. Eli doesn't know how he did it, but he tells Vinnie to consider himself hired under a long term contract, as having these dresses will be enough to pay Pinzolo off immediately. This doesn't please the garment czar, as evidenced by a later conversation between Pinzolo and Vinnie. But Vinnie gets off the hook by saying that if Pinzolo wants him to do something a certain way, he'd better tell him, because he's not a mind reader.

That order of business settled, Vinnie encounters Johnny Coke Bottles on the street, whacks him over the head with his crutch and buries the man in garbage, saying that Pinzolo gave him permission to do so. Johnny makes his way back to his office, immediately puts a call in to Pinzolo, but is interrupted when Frank steps out of the shadows, takes the receiver and tells Pinzolo that Johnny is being arrested.

Vinnie is told by Pinzolo that Johnny must have been arrested by Federal agents, because if it was NYPD he'd know about it, adding that the man could be a dangerous liability. When Johnny ultimately kills himself after Frank convinces him Pinzolo has put a contract out on him (and has failed to get him interested in the Witness Protection Program), Vinnie uses it to his advantage, implying to Pinzolo that he has removed his liability. Pinzolo seems impressed.

"The rag trade was particularly important to me because a part of my family is in the business, and part of that relationship between Eli and David also comes from my own family," explains Stephen Kronish. "So for me, I hated to see that arc end more than any other. In terms of behind the scenes chaos, that was certainly the most angst ridden arc because of Ken's injury."

David Burke adds, "I thought the material in 'Seventh Avenue Freeze Out' was spectacular television. I loved doing that show, and thought it worked very well. One thing the addition of Tony did was blow off the relationship Vinnie would have had with Carol, which would have led Kenny into much different and deeper examinations of the family, and we lost that."

Says director Robert Iscove, "The scenes with Jerry and Ron are incredible. Actually, I liked all of the people we had cast, particularly Patricia Charbonneau and Stanley Tucci. I was trying to give this weasel a contemporary attitude, and something I came up with was his juicer, which we got a lot of mileage out of in terms of humor."

John Schulian does have one complaint about the episode and some of the shows in general. "The speeches were too long," he says, "and a lot of it was self-important hogwash. I think both David Burke and Stephen Kronish are talented, but that a lot of what we did was unnecessarily overblown. The crowning example of that for me, and I think Al Ruggerio, came in this episode, where Vinnie is going to go undercover. David Sternberg goes to the Feds and says, 'We're in trouble. My father went to Rick Pinzolo.' The two guys, Vinnie and David, end up in a fashionable New York disco, with all kinds of good looking women around. These are guys in their prime who should be doing what good looking guys in their prime do in places like that. Instead, we get David Sternberg asking Vinnie, 'Did you

Stanley Tucci as garment industry power broker Rich Pincola

93

love your father?,' and getting weepy talking about his own relationship with Eli. I wanted to throw up. I thought, 'What bullshit. There are not two men on the face of the Earth who are going to have that conversation in that setting that early in their relationship.'"

"Next of Kin"

Original Air Date 12/21/88
Written by Alfonse Ruggerio and John Schulian
Directed by Bill Corcoran

Guest Starring: Jerry Lewis, Ron Silver, Stanley Tucci, Patricia Charbonneau, Anthony Denison, Matthew Walker, David Peterson, Jennifer Griffin, Deryl Hayes, Alex Kliner and Pamela Hart

Vinnie is in the office of Eli Sternberg, and we are introduced to Eli's niece, Carol, who has an obvious attraction to Vinnie, and his brother, Phil. All of them are enroute to an event to honor Pinzolo, but a noise from the street alerts them that someone is stealing a dress from the back of a truck. Everyone runs downstairs, and Vinnie, while chasing the man, is struck by a cab. He is sent to the hospital with broken ribs, a smashed up leg and the like, completely out of commission. Meanwhile, Eli goes to the Pinzolo banquet, has too much to drink and tries to humiliate the man.

Afterwards, Frank, who wrangled an invite to the banquet after Vinnie's injury, visits him in the hospital and is told how badly hurt he really is. He's considering bringing in another agent, and Vinnie wants to know who it could be, because the only reason Pinzolo accepted him was because he has a history that could be bought into. Frank is amused, wanting to know if Vinnie thinks that he's the only one with a history. Before he can answer, Pinzolo approaches the room and Frank goes into hiding. Pinzolo tells Vinnie about what happened at the banquet, and that he wants Eli to desist. Vinnie details the situation of the stolen dress and that Eli thinks he's responsible, at which Pinzolo laughs. He's got his own problems, in that three of his trucks have been hijacked. Why would he waste his time on one dress? What would he gain? Vinnie chalk's Eli's reaction off to a "siege mentality," and points out that Pinzolo's trucking rates are so high, they're crushing Eli. Pinzolo, frankly, doesn't care. Vinnie then adds that he has a partner, who's busy at the moment, but Pinzolo wants him brought in. He leaves the room, Frank steps out of hiding and comments that they've been given the perfect opportunity to bring someone else in. Vinnie doesn't like the idea, but realizes that the situation calls for a desperate action.

To this end, Frank brings in John Henry Raglin, a former OCB operative carrying around his own share of emotional baggage, who has been spending the last few years working in the research department. All we're told is that he and Frank have a kind of history of working together, and that Raglin "did not go out on a winner." This is his opportunity to make amends, and he reluctantly agrees. The first order of business is to see Pinzolo, and tell him that he is taking over for Vinnie, which the man seems to accept.. Then he goes to Elrose, where he finds that Eli is devastated. A terrorist bomb has gone off in the Sri Lanka hotel David was staying in, and he doesn't know whether or not his son is alive. Here we are given a sample of how deeply Eli feels for David, although it's something he never shares with his son. Raglin also gets a sample of the anger and rage Carol feels for her uncle, believing that he stole the business away from her father. Raglin's only reaction is to observe these people, and it's fairly plain that he thinks they're all crazy.

David ultimately turns out to be okay, and Raglin, after earning brownie points with Pinzolo for finding out who has been stealing his trucks (thanks to Frank's stakeouts), goes to see Vinnie in the hospital, telling him he's taken over the assignment. He needs to know everything Vinnie knows.

The most obvious question is how well **Wiseguy** can do without Ken Wahl, the star of the series? Surprisingly, this episode and the next three that make up the rag trade arc prove that the writing is the key to the show. Anthony Denison takes over as John Henry Raglin, and the show doesn't miss a beat. He is terrific, and the character is an instantly intriguing and likeable one. Also, we're presented with the entire main cast from this arc, and there is not a weak performance among them. Jerry Lewis, Ron Silver, Stanley Tucci and Patricia Charbonneau are all tremendous, and the odds are strong that the show will never again bring together an ensemble of actors with as perfect a chemistry as this one.

Notes John Schulian, "With John Henry Raglin we had a chance to create somebody who's entirely different than Vinnie, and who would express the feelings I had and I think Al had. So we get this cold, icy one-line kind of character in him, who when he finally meets the family Sternberg and sees all the neurosis, exposed nerve endings and horse shit, says, 'These people are really sick,' which is exactly the way I felt. He just really hated these people. What was fun is that Denison is such a good actor, we gradually peeled away at his character, which is what should have been done with that show, instead of everyone just coming out and baring their souls."

David Burke explains, "We had two episodes that really had to be thrown out and rewritten because of the absence of Ken, which were 'Next of Kin' and 'All Or Nothing.' 'Where's the Money?' had not been written when Ken was hurt, and we knew we were losing him, so it was a much easier adjustment. I know those two shows would have been better if we had not lost Ken, because there wouldn't have been that crisis rewrite."

Interestingly, for a short time the hope was kept alive that Wahl would return in the middle of the arc, teaming with Denison ala Butch Cassidy and the Sundance Kid.

"All of that was wishful thinking," muses John Schulian. "Ken was a guy who, literally, in the dailies one day we saw collapse. He just couldn't walk. We didn't even know if we were going to be able to take the show beyond that arc, because we thought we might have to fold up shop."

David Burke believes the idea would have played fine, "but Kenny couldn't move at all. We went through two stages. One, we couldn't use Kenny without a partner because of his injury, and then we started wondering about his partner. If he could have a partner who's an older man and who has been down the same path he's been down, he could discover some interesting things. But then it became clear that Kenny couldn't work, so we had to dump all that and come up with a new way to get Raglin involved in this operation."

"All Or Nothing"

Original Air Date 1/11/89

Written by Suzanne Oshry

Directed by Gus Trikonis

Guest Starring: Jerry Lewis, Anthony Denison, Ron Silver, Patricia Charbonneau, Stanley Tucci, Joan Chen, Salem Ludwig and Frederick Neumann

While dealing with his own personal demons, Raglin finds himself walking a tightrope between the Sternbergs and Pinzolo. David, meanwhile, has set up a deal to develop an exact copy, but at a much cheaper rate, of a highly fashionable dress, and it's a deal that is worth millions to Elrose.

Pinzolo, amazingly, wants everything to go through, and will allow nothing to stand in its way, not even a Chinatown strike, which is preventing people from working on the dresses. One woman in particular, Maxine Tzu, is the loudest opponent to the horrible working conditions that exist, and she has encouraged everyone not to return to work until some changes are made. This has Eli terrified, in that without that work force, there is no way his order can go through, and it will result in the ruin of Elrose Fashions.

Raglin becomes involved with Maxine, trying to convince her to listen to what Eli *is* offering her people, saying the changes she wants cannot possibly happen overnight. She is reluctant to consider this, and as she and Raglin have more contact with each other, it's obvious an emotional attraction has been established, culminating in their sleeping together.

All interested parties want this strike to end, and when Maxine's roommate is killed, she recognizes she may be doing more harm than good. She does, however, want to know why *she* wasn't the victim, and Raglin replies that it's because no one wants a martyr. Seeming to understand this, and fearing for the lives of others, she calls off the strike and everyone goes back to work. The changes she has had a role in instigating, though, elevate her to the status of hero in the eyes of her fellow workers.

Both Eli and Pinzolo get what they want: the dresses will be completed on time, and the intrigue continues.

In the midst of shooting the rag trade arc, Jerry Lewis expressed his enthusiasm for the series.

"I don't ordinarily do television," he said, "because I don't like some of the things projected on it. But I've long been a fan of **Wiseguy** for its quality and the caliber of the people involved with it. It's good for the industry when quality is the key word. [Also] the arc is what intrigued me. I would not want to do one-episode television—that's just a brief encounter with your audience. The arc takes the actor into an arena where he can really stretch."

"Where's the Money?"

Original Air Date 1/18/89

Written by David J. Burke and Alfonse Ruggerio Jr.

Directed by Robert Iscove

Guest Starring: Jerry Lewis, Anthony Denison, Ron Silver, Harry Goz, Patricia Charboneau, Stanley Tucci, Tony Ganios, Ken Jenkins and Jennifer M. Evans

The orchestration of the collapse of Elrose Fashions plays out, as bribes at the manufacturing plant insure that the dress material used by Elrose is non-flame retardant.

The dresses the company has been working so hard on are finally in the stores, but when an employee at a shop starts to put one on a mannequin, his lit cigarette sets the material instantly ablaze. He is forced to leap out a window to supposed safety, but breaks his neck in the fall. The next day, the press gets wind of this, Elrose stock plummets, lawsuits fly back and forth and Eli is ruined. As is his wont, he blames David, the one who arranged the original dress deal.

Raglin investigates further, and discovers that Carol Goldman, Eli's niece and Wall Street wizard, has conspired with Pinzolo on inside trading that will allow him to be involved in the eight billion dollar sale of Rightware Department Stores, of which he is a major stockholder. It will allow her to destroy Elrose, her personal goal. She sees it as Biblical retribution for Eli stealing the business from her father. This information is passed on to David, who confronts Carol in her office, shocked beyond belief that his own flesh and blood could betray him in this way. She defends herself, stating she's arranged for ten million dollars of credit in his name,

The legendary Jerry Lewis as Eli Sternberg

97

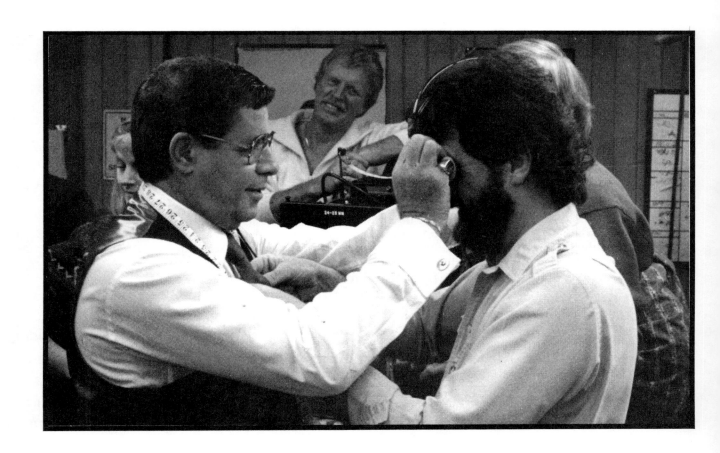

but he couldn't care less. Their confrontation continues a few moments longer. Then David and Raglin depart.

Raglin tries his best to calm David down, stating he may have enough circumstantial evidence to bring Pinzolo to trial, but both realize it's a longshot. And even if the man is found guilty, the penalty will be a slap on the wrist. Raglin asks David to sit tight until he figures out what to do and David agrees, until Raglin has left the building. Then he extracts an envelope from his desk with "1970" written on the front of it, hands it to his Uncle Phil to give Raglin in a couple of days, gets a gun from a drawer and goes to Pinzolo's office, where he tells Ricky they're going to the bank the next morning to extract ten million dollars from his account. Pinzolo agrees, and the next morning he and David go down to the bank to make a withdrawal.

Meanwhile, Raglin has been trying to deal with his personal demons and an undercover assignment that went awry, resulting in the death of an innocent person. It's a memory shared by Frank and new OCB Director Paul Beckstead, who replaced Daryl Elias after the latter was discovered using government phones to place pornographic phone calls terrorizing women. Raglin is eventually contacted by Pinzolo's people, and told they're going to the bank. The next morning he, Frank and other Feds arrive at the same time David and Pinzolo do. There, Pinzolo mentions to David that they're on camera. David is distracted for a moment, and in that instant Pinzolo shoves himself away and screams that David has a gun and it's a robbery. David turns his weapon on Pinzolo, but two of the bank's security guards blow him away. Raglin screams out in horror, and collapses to the floor next to the dead body. He glances up at Pinzolo, who shrugs off David's death, raises his gun and shatters the man's jaw. Raglin gets to his feet and aims his weapon at Pinzolo's head, ready to pull the trigger. Frank talks him down, and later wants him off the case. Obviously, he can't take the emotional pressure, but Raglin swears he's going to see it through.

At the hospital, a devastated Eli identifies David's body, and as he enters the corridor, he sees Pinzolo walking out of another room. Pinzolo's doctor says that his jaw is wired in such a way that he'll be on liquids for a couple of weeks. At that moment, Eli swings out and punches him in the jaw, sending Pinzolo to the floor in excruciating pain.

"Gee, Ricky," notes McPike wryly, "guess you're going to need some more wiring."

"I was so exhausted at the time, that it's tough to remember much of the episode," says David Burke. "It was like, 'Steve, is that show done?' 'Yeah, I took care of it. You took care of 'Where's the Money?,' right?' 'Yeah.' Somehow we survived, and I do think that Stanley Tucci was great. I remember that much. In 'Where's the Money?' there's a scene where Ron Silver's got a gun on him and Stanley absolutely steals the scene, despite the fact that Ron is spectacular. Jesus, to get those two guys together...it will probably always be my favorite arc, because we survived it.

In his own inimitable way, Jerry Lewis goofs around behind the scenes

"We do try to deal with stuff that goes on in the world on a day-to-day basis," he continues. "I'm real interested in how we function as a society, and there's a line in 'Where's the Money?' where Ron Silver mentions NASA and the O-rings. I wrote that and somebody said, 'Gee, should we really be attacking NASA?' I thought for a minute and said, 'Damn right we should. We should hold everybody's feet to the flame,' including our own. These people should care about what they do in the same way that I care about what I do. There was a speech in one episode about the responsibility the individual has to take for the behavior of society, and that, to me, is the crux of what we write about. If you're not willing to take it on yourself, you really can't blame anybody else for what happens. Maybe that's why the unwashed don't watch us, because they don't want to hear statements like that."

Robert Iscove says, "As great as Denison was, Kenny has an edge and a way of playing the character that we were trying to search out for Tony all the way through. We finally got to it by 'Where's the Money?,' but it was really a matter of searching out who the character is and what his relationship with all of this stuff is."

Adds John Schulian, "Since the time that **Wiseguy** has been on the air, there have been two all-time great scenes. The first of course was Vinnie and Sonny beating the piss out of each other in the theatre, and Sonny turning himself into a french fry. The other one is when Raglin goes to Carol Sternberg and tells her how David died. She says, 'Did he suffer?' And Raglin says, 'Did he suffer? I really can't tell you,' all the while pressing his finger against her forehead. Writing on television doesn't get any better, and you know what? It was graphic, and that scene probably would not get on the air on an NBC show. CBS really, I guess because they have so many other fires to put out, let us have a lot of freedom. I think it makes the show better, to a point. You can't give just anybody freedom. Part of the thing that drove me nuts about the show are the very things that give it its energy and make it quirky and special."

"Postcard From Morrocco"

Original Air Date 1/25/89

Written by Stephen Kronish, John Schulian and Alfonse Ruggerio Jr.

Directed by Roy Campanella II

Guest Starring: Jerry Lewis, Anthony Denison, Harry Goz, Patricia Charboneau, Stanley Tucci, Tony Ganios, Sheila Paterson, Dwight Koss, Kevin McNulty, Pamela Hart, Dale Robins and Sid Filkow

At David's funeral, Eli, whose second wife has left him because his money is gone, offers Raglin his final $50,000 if he'll eliminate Pinzolo. Naturally Raglin refuses, choosing instead to follow possible leads that will get Pinzolo indicted.

It begins with the letter David had left him; a letter which details David and Pinzolo supplying drugs to the "Woodstock Generation" some twenty years earlier and that Pinzolo murdered one of his distribution people. The letter details exactly where they buried the body, but further investigation turns up no evidence as a building has been constructed over the site. Next, Raglin turns his attention to Carol Goldman, who obviously fears Pinzolo may want to cause her harm because of her knowledge. Raglin talks to her about the Witness Protection Program, which half his family is supposedly in. Carol ultimately agrees to get evidence and testify.

Meanwhile, Eli comes to Pinzolo's office, holding him at bay by gunpoint. He makes Rick beg to have his life spared, which he does, a fact which gives Eli great deal pleasure. Then Frank shows up, and eventually talks Eli into handing over his weapon. Pinzolo doesn't want to press charges. He just wants Frank to get this "old man" out of his office.

Later, Pinzolo begins liquidating his assets, wanting to take his money and the twenty million he made from the Rightware sale and escape to Morrocco, where he'll be beyond the reach of the law. At the same time, Carol comes to see him, they make love and she wants to get some of the Rightware money for her silence. Pinzolo offers her 32% of what he made, and she accepts, but then he finds a hidden tape recorder in her pocketbook, realizes she's betrayed him and strangles her to death. The body is shipped off, and eventually found by the OCB, but there is no link to Pinzolo.

It all concludes at an airport in Buffalo, as Pinzolo is about to board his private jet. Raglin arrives, fires his gun in the air and stops Pinzolo in his tracks. Pinzolo wants to know what he wants. He offers him his trucking company, which will

Accusations fly back and forth between Eli Sternberg and Rick Pincola

make Raglin the king of 7th Avenue. He has no interest at all. Then Frank arrives, and confidence swells in Pinzolo, as he says, "Take him, McPike. You're a cop!"

"So am I!" is Raglin's passionate response.

Pinzolo is stunned for a moment, but then starts to laugh as he puts two and two together, and realizes that Terranova must be a cop as well, a fact which will interest quite a few friends of his. He approaches his plane, turns and his gloved hand gives the impression of a gun. Raglin whirls, fires and a bullet strikes Pinzolo in the heart. He collapses lifelessly to the ground.

The episode concludes with Raglin stating this case has finally allowed him to put the demons of his mind to rest, and now provides him with the opportunity to leave the OCB. Two good friends say goodbye, and Raglin's next stop is Elrose, and Eli Sternberg who sits in his sewing room, a ruined man, contemplating what's left of his life. The two men say goodbye to each other. Eli shares observations he has made since David's death about life and himself, and the rag trade arc comes to an end.

"What I liked about 'Postcard From Morrocco' was that we finally find out what had happened to Raglin," explains John Schulian, "that this guy was tortured and that he gave up people and they were killed. That he has borne all this guilt for all of these years. This is his one way to try and make amends, and we wrapped it all up at the airport where he killed Pinzolo. Then there's that wonderful tag where you see Eli sitting at the sewing machine, which is exactly the way we began the arc, only this time he's a broken man."

Adds Stephen Kronish, "The final scene between Raglin and Pinzolo was an effective one, and I have to give a tremendous tip of the hat to Denison and Stanley Tucci. Tucci is one of the best actors around and he was tremendous in that arc. The way I had originally written it, is that there had been no shots fired until Raglin killed him. They were out there playing it at the airport, and they called me at night and said, 'Can we fire twice before we shoot him?' They gave me their reasons why, and it sounded like it made sense. I told them to go ahead, and it worked much better than what I had originally written.

"I also liked the last scene between Jerry and Denison, where Denison comes into the sewing room and Jerry gives this speech where he says he's been thinking about his father, and saying that 'All the things I've done, basically, I deluded myself into thinking it was for David and his mother, but that was a lie.' It was Jerry Lewis' most effective moment. There was some discussion as to whether or not Eli should live through this. I felt strongly, and I was able to persuade other people, that since we had killed David, and rather than making this show *Hamlet* where everybody's dead, we should leave Eli alive. Leaving him sitting alone in that room amidst the sewing machines and ghosts of his son and everything they had built over the last 40 years, was more emotionally effective than having him jump out a building or putting a bullet through his head.

"That final speech I had written just sort of came out right, and it was enhanced by Jerry's playing it the way he did, which was just to say the words without acting. That really worked out well. There aren't many times when you can watch your own stuff and get emotionally moved by it, because you know it so well and you know what it took to put it down on paper, but that was a moment where I got a little choked up when I heard him saying those things. If I had to pick one of the big moments I had written that had affected me, that would be number one."

The rag trade arc was a wonderful rebound from the lackluster reaction given to the white supremacy storyline by the show's staff. They had taken the adversity of their leading man's absence, and channeled it into a success that was stunning in its effectiveness. Unfortunately, as they and the fans of **Wiseguy** can attest, the next arc would prove considerably weaker, as a full season of trying to beat the production clock finally caught up to the writing staff, and exhaustion set in.

*Stanley
Tucci*

RON SILVER

Perhaps one of the major casting coups in **Wiseguy's** *history came during the rag trade arc, when Jerry Lewis was signed to portray Eli Sternberg, and Ron Silver was pegged to portray his son, Eli. The chemistry between the two was apparent from their first scene together. There was no problem buying into this father/son relationship.*

Prior to joining the show, Silver, who had acquired a wide variety of credits on stage and in film, had completed the one-two punch of starring on Broadway in David Mamet's critically acclaimed "Speed the Plow," and before the cameras in Kathryn Bigalow's Blue Steel.

I got a call from David Burke, who's an old acquaintance/friend of mine, and we'd lost touch. He called me up and told me he was doing **Wiseguy**, but I'm not a TV watcher so I'd never seen the show; I hadn't seen a lot of shows. He asked me to take a look at it, and I said, "Look, I'm just coming off of a Broadway show and there are a couple of things I want to do, and I don't think I'll have time," and so forth. David kept saying, "Take a look at the show," and he sent me some tapes with other friends like Ray Sharkey, Kevin Spacey, and they were just terrific. The show seemed a little different and it seemed like fun, but I still wasn't that interested. I had just done "Speed the Plow" on Broadway and I did a film called *Blue Steel*. I was working kind of non-stop, which is enviable for an actor, but I'm lazy too and would like to spend time with my family. This was in November or December, and David got on the phone and said, "We'd love you to come to Vancouver for eight weeks to do it. We do these things called arcs, and you would be in like five or six shows." I told him I like to spend November and December home with my family, and he said, "Just read the script." He sent the script, I read it and thought it was very good, and then he called and told me Jerry Lewis was signed to play the father. So I heard Jerry Lewis, and now I had more of a decision to make than I thought. The script was good, the show was good and I was dying to work with Jerry Lewis. So I called David up, and I was really difficult. I was very selfish and I wanted everything to go my way. There was no negotiations about money or anything, because everybody was getting the same thing and it was fairly generous, but I just made what I thought were unreasonable demands. The reason I made them is that I wouldn't have been happy doing the show unless they were met. It really had to do with my time. If I was up there, I really wanted to come home for Thanksgiving and spend ten days at home. Then I didn't want to work for the Chanukah and Christmas holiday, and they agreed. That's how I got involved, and I'm terribly glad that I did get involved, because I like the work, I loved working with David and I like Cannell's operation up there.

Working with Jerry was everything I wanted it to be and more. There was also Stanley Tucci, Pat Charbonneau, all the people were terrific. The directors were good. David Burke was very involved and they made us feel very much a part of the team. They were interested in our input, they listened to us when they thought we were right, there wasn't a lot of ego driving the thing and it was a real thrill for me from beginning to end working with Jerry. The whole thing turned out so delightful, that in retrospect part of me is sorry I made the demands about coming back, because to accommodate me they had to write me out of episodes two and three. They had me killed, at my suggestion, in episode four, but it was so good that I wish I had schlepped my family there. Originally I was supposed to be more heavily involved in episodes two and three and I wasn't supposed to die. I suggested they kill me at the end of episode four, because I had to be home and there was no other way to write me out. I collaborated somewhat on the script and some of the scenes and spoke to David about it, and that's what they did, because, contractually, they had no choice. I know it sounds kind of saccharine, but I really didn't have any adversarial relationships up there. The thing was delightful from beginning to end.

They weren't quite sure (what they were going to do with David before I suggested they kill him). They hadn't written the episodes yet. They had a range of options from Jerry being knocked off to God knows what. There were also problems up there, because Kenny hurt his foot and they were scrambling. They did a remarkable job of adjusting by getting Tony Denison in, who's a terrific guy as well. I am sorry that I didn't get to know Ken better than I did, because he was terrific the first week and quite heroic trying to make this work when he was experiencing a lot of pain. So they were scrapping and rewriting scripts to adjust for this new character. It was a fairly chaotic time, and we went on hiatus for three or four days there.

The writing on the show is good and they're willing to take chances. I find that people in the movie industry and perhaps in the TV industry, too, are so afraid because nobody knows what makes something a success, and if everything gels and it's successful, they're afraid to touch any element because they don't know what it is. It's like actors getting laughs in a show and there are two guys up there. Later one of them says, "When I said this the audience really laughed," and the other guy says, "Yeah, but while you're saying that, I'm doing this," so then they experiment and each one doesn't do it that night and there's no laugh. Then they say, "Okay, let's go back to what we had," and it's gone. I guess they'll usually attribute it to the actor, but was *10* a success because of Dudley Moore? If it was, why wasn't his next six movies a success? The same thing with Richard Gere. He scored in *An Officer and a Gentleman*, but what happened to his other films? So who knows? I don't know if it's Kenny, although I'm sure he's attractive to a lot of people. I do know that the writing is awfully good, and they can attract pretty good actors because they write wonderful parts. I'll go wherever the work is good. I'll even do a fabulous off-off-Broadway play. This was better than a movie because you were dealing with the same character, and I knew we were dealing with a five hour movie. It's like doing a really good miniseries. In the arc form, you don't have to really compress that much. One episode could be wasted on little nice, rich, luxuriant behavioral things that really didn't move the story forward, because I had four or five hours to do that. If you can use the form, TV, like they do, then it can be something quite wonderful. They also have a great supporting team over there, Jim Byrnes and Jonathan Banks. They're terrific, and I just had a real good time.

A lot of people ask what I think of the characters I'm playing, and the most honest answer is that I really don't think about it. I do a lot of research and preparation, not necessarily because I'm a perfectionist, but because I like that part of the work. I like finding out things. But I don't get judgmental about them, because if I do it makes it hard for me to play them. If I have a strong opinion of like or dislike or I've analyzed their motives too much, it becomes very hard to *be* them. I know a lot of people like the Sternbergs. My father was peripherally involved in the garment trade. He worked for a sportswear company in middle management. A lot of work I didn't have to do, because I knew people like them.

There were a couple of things going on. Jerry Lewis is about the same age as my father, and not terribly dissimilar in terms of physical appearance. From the time I was five years old, Jerry Lewis was a star. I remember seeing him and whenever somebody my age did something funny, we were flattered when they'd say, "Oh, you remind me of Jerry Lewis." So I've been living with this guy since five years old, and when I got to meet him there was an immediate rapport between the both of us. It was very easy for us to fall into a father and son relationship. We both have a tremendous respect for each other and we got along tremendously. He was very generous with his time, and almost every night we were there we would have dinner together, and that was over a period of six or seven weeks. We didn't do that because it was good for the work. We did it because we enjoyed each other's company and we had a lot to talk about that evening. We didn't talk about the work.

The thing that sticks out in my mind is that the actors were treated like adults. They had contributions to make. They were not hired just to say the words. They are encouraged to have input, and for an actor such as myself, that's important. I would assume it's important to a lot of other actors as well. They all labor together to make a working environment that's designed for optimal creativity, and that's reflected on the show.

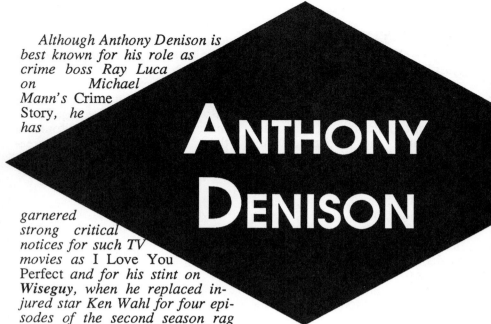

ANTHONY DENISON

Although Anthony Denison is best known for his role as crime boss Ray Luca on Michael Mann's Crime Story, *he has garnered strong critical notices for such TV movies as* I Love You Perfect *and for his stint on* Wiseguy, *when he replaced injured star Ken Wahl for four episodes of the second season rag trade storyline.*

It goes back to my days on *Crime Story*. When I started on that show, a friend of mine—a good friend of min— David Burke, started as the story editor. He left mid-way through the first year, but we remained very good friends. He then went on to work on **Wiseguy**. This past October, I was doing a TV movie and when I finished, on the last day he called and said, "Ken Wahl hurt his foot, would you mind coming up and being the wiseguy? We'll figure out the storyline and we'll fit you in. We're really in a jam." Well, David is my good friend, so I didn't think anything of it.

They're good writers, the whole staff, and I wasn't fearful. My biggest fear was just making sure that I would do as good a job as possible, to justify the confidence and enthusiasm they had with me doing the part. That was my biggest fear, and not so much what they were going to supply to me, because they write very well.

Every role you play is tough. I don't know how to put it, but you want to go in and try to do the best job that you can. Sometimes it doesn't work out, whether you're going in to replace somebody or whether you're going in fresh. I literally landed on Tuesday night and found myself on the set Wednesday morning, and the first scene that you saw me in on the show was the first scene that I shot. The confusion and the distance that everyone felt my character had in that scene was real, because I was unsure. So it was convenient, in a sense, and great that I was able to use my uncertainty, my, "Gee, what's going on?" hurly burly kind of thing, and use it toward the character. Then it was just a question of getting to know everybody.

Jonathan Banks was just wonderful. He was like a rock for me, and a great guy to work with. Jerry Lewis, Ron Silver, Stanley Tucci, Patricia Charbonneau, who I knew from *Crime Story*, it was just great and everybody was just so helpful and wonderful. Also, my wife got to play my wife on the show. When I went up there, I said, "If the wife plays an important part in his background, why not have her show up? And why not have it be my real life wife? She's an actress." David said, "Sure," and we did.

A lot of people go through life and try certain things and they don't work out. You walk around saying, "What if?" A lot of times you don't get a second chance, but when you do, and it presents itself, it's very fortunate. Here John Raglin had a second chance. When Jonathan Banks' character says that he didn't go out on a win, here was an opportunity for him to go out on a win. He's getting a second chance at it, which is great and everyone in life should have a chance at it. Sometimes people will present it to you, and sometimes you'll have to make it happen yourself. When it does come you have a chance to redeem yourself.

I used exactly what they wrote. I didn't try to improve on their stuff, because if it's not broke, don't fix it. They showed this guy getting a second chance and how he's trying to walk the tightrope and do it the way he used to, like a circus performer. When the rope was a little wobbly, you could see him stopping, figuring it out, figuring it out, figuring it out, and then he's able to get to the other side. He does, and once he's there, he says, "I don't need to be on the tightrope anymore, but I needed to do it one more time." He didn't have to go back, which is why at the end he says, "I don't know where I'm going, but I know it's out of this nonsense."

It was easy to play what they gave me, plus I trusted David as a friend and a writer. They were all aware of that. They asked me on a Thursday to do this, Saturday I was in their office meeting with David, Al Ruggerio, John Schulian. We discussed different aspects of the character, and then on Sunday David and I spoke some more, did some more talking on Monday, trying to work out who he would be. I left Tuesday and Wednesday I was on the set. They literally had to rewrite the whole script by Tuesday. The other problem was that they didn't know how bad off Ken was. They thought maybe they could still keep Ken Wahl in the story, and have him be in a hospital bed, in which case Ken Wahl and I would talk about the case and what to do with me visiting him in the hospital. Then by the last episode we might be working together as a kind of Butch Cassidy and the

Sundance Kid, where he thinks I'm this washed up agent but realizes why I was so good. We work together in the end, and then I say, "Take it easy kid," and ride off into the sunset. That was the original plan, but Ken's foot was in such bad shape the doctor's report was that he should stay off it for at least six weeks. They didn't even want to take the risk of bringing him to the set.

On television they have their TV movies, which are produced very quickly, in about a month, whereas a film takes two months to shoot. A miniseries is a television version of a feature film. They really go out on them, spending a lot more time shooting. Not as much as they would a feature film, but they spend time. So the deal is when you do a TV series and get the opportunity to play the same character over six hours or five hours, it's the same thing as doing a miniseries. It gives you the opportunity to really deal and delve into your character and come up with the characterization that plays out over those episodes, if it's not something that's done for the quick results. You can sort of feel through it, and it's a wonderful opportunity for an actor. It's the next best thing to doing a miniseries or to working a film.

It really depends on how well written it is; it's the strength of the words on the page that it gets down to. You've got to start with a good script. Once you get a coherent script, then you as the actor can have a ball. It could be a comedy, or a really heavy involved drama where the tightrope goes out emotionally. Now Luca (his character on *Crime Story*) was a good character, there were a lot of times where locations and the staff were being changed, that you had to safeguard your own character. Again, since we didn't go with the arc aspect, you really have to safeguard yourself. As John Henry Raglin, it was the arc so you had the opportunity to see the beginning, middle and end with the character. Actually, the very first year of *Crime Story*, we had a

bible...whereas **Wiseguy** is a six or seven hour little movie, *Crime Story* was a 22 hour movie; one continuous story through the season. Because of this bible, which outlined all 22 stories, I knew from the beginning to the end what my character would do, which is wonderful. You get an opportunity to then plan and really delve into different aspects of the character, because you know that eventually he's going to be here, how he gets here and why. Emotionally you bring that to it. The second year of *Crime Story* we didn't have that bible, and it was episode by episode. It became more episodic. The first year was the first time that there was a serialized episodic show. The characters remained the same. Torilla

as still chasing Luca, but in the meantime there were different people that entered both storylines, so you were able to keep the integrity of the serial, but at the same time introduce new characters. To have them come and go and play out the whole scenario. The second year, that didn't work out as successfully.

I would like to say that I had a great time (working on **Wiseguy**). It's a wonderful crew, they really work hard. They were very supportive. The whole Cannel organization and CBS really treated me like royalty, and I welcome the opportunity to work on a CBS movie or miniseries in the future, or with Cannell again. They were just wonderful.

Season Two
INNER DEMONS

"Stairway to Heaven"
Original Air Date 2/1/89
Written by Alfonse Ruggerio Jr.
Directed by James Contner
Guest Starring: Ken Jenkins, David Wilson and Jessica Harper

Frank shows up at Vinnie's house practically in tears, saying that his wife, Jenny, is going to die unless she has a liver transplant. The problem is that she's an alcoholic, and not high on the priority list in terms of donors. In addition, the operation costs upwards of $100,000 and Frank simply doesn't have that kind of money.

Vinnie, who is still on crutches, popping pain killers and talking about his own set of demons, tries to provide aid in the form of $1,250,000, a part of the cash given to him by Roger Loccoco who had obtained it from Mel Profitt's organization as the finances needed for the aborted military coup of Isle Pavot. Frank is resistant to use what may be drug money, despite Vinnie's argument that he should put the money to some good use. Ultimately Frank agrees, giving the hospital enough for the operation and the balance as a donation. He tries to turn himself over to OCB for misuse of government funds, but Paul Beckstead tells him that the Profitt and Loccoco cases are closed with no loose ends, so therefore the money doesn't exist. Frank has been a good friend and a good operative for the OCB. There's no need to make mention of this situation.

The donation moves Jenny up the list, and she gets the needed liver. Ironically, while she's recovering from the operation, she gains a new outlook on life: she wants a divorce from Frank, because, as she notes, "This marriage cost me a liver. Now you've given me one back. Let's call it even."

At episode's end, Frank plugs a bullet into a jukebox playing "Hit the Road, Jack," gets frustrated at a sleazy hotel when he hears a couple making passionate love in the next room, and shows up at Vinnie's house, needing a place to stay.

"The four shows that followed 'Postcard From Morocco' were very important to me," says David Burke. "'Stairway to Heaven', which was a McPike show, is one of them. Alfonse Ruggerio wrote it and we all knew that we had to keep Kenny off his feet. Since he had the millions of dollars from Roger Loccoco in his closet, I feel we got away with that, although a lot of people objected to it. There's like two and a half acts of he and McPike arguing with each other whether or not it's right that they have the mon

Vinnie encounters his recently departed brother
in a WISEGUY nightmare sequence

ey and what to do with it. And then he saves his wife and she says, 'Thank you very much, get out of the house.'"

"I've got to tell you, when we did 'Stairway to Heaven,' it was a hard choice for us at the end when Frank shot the juke box as 'Hit the Road, Jack' came on," smiles Les Sheldon. "It made us laugh, because it was him being so frustrated. There's no question that we went over the top with it, but so does a human being in that situation. When we see a human being go over the top, we'll go right with him. I think that's what makes our show as entertaining as it is."

"White Noise"

Original Air Date 2/15/89

Written by David J. Burke, Story by Ken Wahl

Directed by James Whitmore Jr.

Guest Starring: Ray Sharkey, Gerald Anthony, John M. Jackson, Ken Jenkins and David Schramm

Frank remains concerned over Vinnie's continual use of crutches and constant pill taking. He and Paul insist that Vinnie undergo a physical, or retire. He opts for the former, but unbeknownst to him, Daryl Elias is in the hospital as well for psychological evaluation. When he finds out that Vinnie's there, he goes into the hospital's computer and alters Terranova's records so that they indicate he's dangerously psychotic.

Vinnie is restrained, drugged and generally abused by the hospital staff, none of whom will pay the slightest bit of attention to his claim of being a Federal officer. The worst is yet to come, however, as he slips into a drugged state and is forced to face the darkest nightmare of his soul: Sonny Steelgrave. In several highly surrealistic dream sequences, Vinnie faces Sonny's accusations of betrayal, and finally comes to grips with the man's *evil*, and that the time has finally come for him to get the gnawing at the pit of his stomach out of his system. He has to go forward with life, without the emotional baggage his experience with Sonny brought.

A fellow inmate hears Vinnie screaming out Lifeguard's number and makes a phone call, which leads Frank to the psychiatric ward. Once freed, Vinnie knocks out the head doctor, and arrests Patrick, one of the orderlies, who is charged with assaulting a Federal Agent.

David Burke admits that this episode, "was the only time I thought we were taking a chance, because I had steadfastedly refused to bring Ray Sharkey back. But he had so much fun and was always asking me to do it, and it finally just rolled around in our collective psyche that we could do it, and we went with it.

"Kenny and I had been sitting around talking and the idea for 'White Noise' came up," he elaborates. "I said, 'You know, I get weird letters all the time about bringing Ray Sharkey back. Why don't we bring that character back and let's say Vinnie has the same problems that the audience has, because they did like Ray and Sonny Steelgrave. Let's bring this guy back and show that he's this little gnawing feeling in Vinnie's gut, and let's call a spade a spade. Let's say who this guy is,'

Left: Ray Sharkey returns from the grave as Sonny Steelgrave to haunt the subconscious mind of Vinnie
Below: The final moment between Vinnie and Sonny Steelgrave as Vinnie exorcises his personal demon

SEASON TWO
M U S I C

Perhaps the most fascinating aspect of the music industry arc is that at its outset most of the producers laboring on the show truly believed it would consist of some of the best episodes of **Wiseguy** ever produced. By the time the cycle came to an end seven shows later, they were deemed among the worst.

In early 1989, the author had spoken to several of the principals involved behind the scenes, and it's interesting to compare their initial enthusiasm to the comments made by them some seven months later. Les Sheldon had been approached first, asked to detail which arc, in his estimation, was the best.

"In what respect?" he asked rhetorically. "Everything is so different. At first people thought we were a mob show, then they realized we weren't. Then we got into the garment district, now we're starting in the music business. It's not about the mob. It's about different human beings who have gone wrong. As far as an overall arc, it may be the music arc. We've got some really interesting people in it, and some powerful stuff is starting to come out of the typewriters. This could be the strongest one overall. Sometimes the strengths come from the weaknesses we explore. That's what I think makes our show so interesting. We explore the flaws of human beings, and in fact some of them are weak and misguided. They're not fluff. Each arc we go in a different direction."

John Schulian had noted at the time, "I'm real enthused about this arc. We're looking at a world that's unlike any that we've ever seen, and Vinnie does not have to be pulled into it, because he's very eager to investigate the music industry. This gives him the opportunity to briefly run his own record company, which ultimately gets swallowed by a larger company owned by Paul Winfield and then Tim Curry. The idea is that the industry is wall-to-wall corruption and Vinnie is going to sink one of the big boys. We're not interested in payola, but we are looking at cleans—which is the counterfeiting of records, cut out scams, defrauding artists and things like that. This stuff was there before we started and I'm afraid it's going to be here long after the last episode has run. But it is a fascinating industry, and the arc is filled with these wonderful characters."

David Burke was equally enthused, believing the storyline would open up an entirely new arena for the characterization of Terranova.

"Vinnie's much more in control of things," he said. "He's not someone's lackey, like he was with Sonny and Mel Profitt. He's in the driver's seat and that's a lot of fun to play around with. It's a wild and wacky world, and it's going to be a much different show than it's been in the past. Vinnie's going to be in a suit and tie a lot more because he's working as an executive, and his experience with Sonny and Mel Profitt has trained him and taught him about the wheeling and dealings of big business. Now he has all the facilities to function as those men did, and he's going to bring those talents to this arc."

Tim Curry as Winston Newquay, chief villain of WISEGUY's fifth story arc

"Dead Dog Lives"

Original Air Date 3/1/89

Written by David J. Burke and Stephen Kronish

Directed by Gus Trikonis

Guest Starring: Glenn Frey, Deborah Harry, Pamela Segall, Paul McCrane and Ken Jenkins

In an attempt to investigate the music industry, Vinnie Terranova is named president of Dead Dog Records, a label whose assets were seized by the Federal government.

No sooner has he sat down behind his desk than Bobby Travis enters his office. A man with incredible contacts in the music industry, Travis was one step away from purchasing Dead Dog when Vinnie suddenly came out of nowhere and beat him to the punch. Ultimately Vinnie hires him and begins a crash course on the business. This leads to a small bar where Diana Price, once a musical giant, with 40 million records sold, who is under contract to Dead Dog, is playing to relatively unenthusiastic crowds. Vinnie senses her appeal right away, and wants to get her to record a new single. Bobby doesn't think it's a good idea, because as much as he respects and cares for her (they're old friends), he feels her time has passed. Diana is tentatively interested at best, fearful of failure.

Travis' contacts combined with Vinnie's bold moves lands them with legendary record producer Johnny Medley, a character who was probably inspired by Phil Spector. They hire Medley to produce Diana's new single "Brite Side"—if they can convince Diana that recording again is a good idea.

Eventually they're successful. They go into the studio and after some initial mishaps with the extremely temperamental Medley, produce a demo recording.

"Dead Dog Lives" is a solid episode, effectively bringing Vinnie into the music industry and hooking him up with an assortment of characters, some more bizarre than others. Perhaps most enjoyable is that it takes the character of Vinnie Terranova into a whole new arena completely unlike what we've seen before.

"I love that episode," laughs David Burke, "because when Frank gives him this assignment, Vinnie's thrilled with it, which scares the hell out of Frank. He gets to see Vinnie operate in a world he has fun in, and he's dealing with a bunch of children—some of whom are lethal. To see him master that world in 'Dead Dog Lives' was fun for us. There was a lot of good feeling on that show. That arc did, however, get away from us, because the network was so thrilled with the Jerry Lewis episodes that they suddenly wanted us to use celebrities, and we caved in to that without any fight. It was okay, but we got so many actors that we couldn't service any of them the way we should have. The Bobby Travis character played out well for us, and Isaac Twine was terrific and so was Johnny Medley. Winston Newquay was terrific, but the rest just didn't work. We got so jammed with characters that it became impossible to manage the arc, so it was a relief when it was over."

THE MAKING OF A WISEGUY

Top Left: Deidre Hall as Claudia Newquay, Winston's wife

Bottom Left: Paul Winfield portrays record mogul Isaac Twine

Top Right: Debbie Harry is Diana Price, musician seeking a comeback via Vinnie's OCB financed Dead Dog Records

Bottom Right: Mick Fleetwood makes a powerful cameo appearance

One point John Schulian brings out is that the staff was worried about singer turned actor Glenn Frey. "The first day of dailies we were really nervous about him, because his acting only consisted of a *Miami Vice* episode and a movie called *Let's Get Harry*. That first day, though, we said, 'This guy's golden.' He was just tremendous."

"And It Comes Out Here"

Original Air Date 3/8/89
Written by David J. Burke and Stephen Kronish
Directed by Bill Corcoran

Guest Starring: Glenn Frey, Deborah Harry, Pamela Segall, Paul McCrane, Paul Winfield, Patti D'Arbanville, Tim Curry, Deidre Hall, Mick Fleetwood and Ken Jenkins

With the "Brite Side" demo in tow, Vinnie and Travis start shopping Diana Price around. Vinnie's personal agenda is to hook Dead Dog up with a larger label, thus getting closer to the source of his investigation. First stop is Isaac Twine and Shakala Records. When they enter his office, Isaac's in the middle of watching a wrestling match. Once it's over, he calls ruthless music power broker Winston Newquay to gloat over winning their bet. He cuts the conversation short and turns his attention to Vinnie and Travis.

While saying he enjoyed "Brite Side," he thinks it would be too expensive to promote. Vinnie notes that the Diana Price album is not the only item on the block: for $4.5 million, Isaac can have the complete Dead Dog catalog, Diana Price and independent contracts for the two of them. Isaac is tempted, but he doesn't really have the capital.

Next stop is Winston Newquay, perhaps the most powerful man in the music industry, who also happens to have been Diana Price's lover some ten years earlier. He has the power to make or break careers and succinctly states he has no interest in what they're offering.

That night, Newquay throws a party for a Soviet musician he's just signed under contract, and the party is crashed by Travis, Vinnie and Diana. Travis announces to the attending press that Diana is returning to the world of music. All of this is watched by Newquay's wife, Claudia, who is furious that Diana is there, as she remains threatened by the woman her husband once had an affair with. In fact, the two women actually get into a fight, which results in their crashing into the buffet table.

Bobby and Vinnie then meet with James Elliot, a music superstar whose accomplishments sound like those of Elvis and the Beatles *combined*. The duo want him to sign with Dead Dog for the resulting publicity, a fact Elliot recognizes and doesn't mind. In fact when he hears Vinnie's terms ("I don't want you to record or anything. All I want you to do is consult with me once a month....telepathically."), he has no problems signing, since he hates Newquay. He even calls Winston to rub it in his face.

The next day, Newquay offers eleven million dollars for Dead Dog, minus Diana Price, Travis and Vinnie. Vinnie refuses, electing to sign with Shakala for no money down, which saddens Travis beyond words.

Things aren't all rock and roll, as Newquay has used a political contact to access Vinnie's file, and received information pertaining to his cover. Frank points out that if he digs any deeper, he just may discover that Vinnie is a Federal officer.

Things are still going well by episode two of the arc, as the introduction of characters continues. Tim Curry is outstanding as that villain of villains Winston Newquay, and Paul Winfield continues in his extremely likeable role of Isaac Twine. The viewer does, however, start to get the sense of too many players, but it isn't overwhelming yet.

"When I came over to *Midnight Caller* this year," says John Schulian, "one of the writers on the show, who has worked in the music industry for a long time, said that the one thing lacking in the music arc was music. That gets into money. You can't afford to pay $25,000 every week, so we could not have a lot of tunes in the background. This is a classic example of the kind of thing that happened on the show. Kronish never liked the arc from the get-go and Burke just lost interest in it and let it peter out. They liked elements of it, and obviously they liked Patti D'Arbanville, because they kept her around, which I think was a mistake. She's a fine actress, but I don't think there's anything going on between her and Ken Wahl. There was never any magic there, and that's not the kind of girl Vinnie Terranova would go for. But if you talk about good actors and wonderful characters, you had Paul McCrane as Johnny Medley. He was just wonderfully out of his mind, going face first into a bowl of gumbo. That was a classic Burke scene, because he really has a wonderful flair for those great, memorable outrageous scenes, and that's one where Medley's tooted up and drunk, pulling a gun on Vinnie and Bobby Travis. Then Vinnie looks at Bobby and says, 'This guy's crazy. We're screwed.' And Glenn says, 'What do you mean? We're going to be great.'"

"The Rip Off Stick"

Original Air Date 3/22/89

Written by Stephen Kronish and David J. Burke

Directed by Mario Azzopardi

Guest Starring: Glenn Frey, Deborah Harry, Pamela Segall, Peter Williams, Paul McCrane, Paul Winfield, Patti D'Arbanville, Tim Curry, Deirdre Hall, Ken Jenkins, Paul Garrett, Billy Wirth, Peter Yunker and Ron Taylor

Vinnie gets a phone call from Monroe Blue, a songwriter who is under contract to Dead Dog. He's been arrested for breaking into a jukebox and stealing the money, in retribution for the fact that Winston Newquay hasn't paid him any royalties on an extremely popular number. The man is looking for work, and he's more than happy to have Vinnie and Travis line things up for him.

At a party for Diana Price, Winston shows up with rock and roll star Eddie Tempest, and tries every trick in the book to get him on stage when Diana herself is late for the event, a fact which doesn't bother Claudia Newquay at all. She does eventually show up and performs "Brite Side" live, which gets the crowd rocking and rolling. After the evening, though, things take a turn for the worse when she gets into a waiting limo, and Newquay is within. She succumbs to the feelings she still has for him, and the two make love.

Meanwhile, Vinnie is freaking because he discovers that supposedly unsold records he's being billed for are actually not what they seem to be, resulting in a bill for $57,000 for bogus merchandise. He is completely furious, and Frank points out to him that he's taking things too seriously. Considering this for a moment, he agrees, recognizing that he was looking at the situation as a record executive rather than a cop.

Later, Diana Price has a meeting with Vinnie and Travis, telling them that she slept with Newquay, and that she has to get away or she'll fall completely under his control again, and will sign with him once her current contract runs out. If she has time to write her own songs, maybe that will provide enough of a power base to stand on her own. And so she disappears, infuriating Newquay, who demands to know where she is, but gets no answer.

"'The Rip Off Stick' introduced us to Monroe Blue," says John Schulian. "He was wonderful, Ron Taylor, who had been the voice of the man eating plant in *Little Shop of Horrors* on Broadway. Just terrific. His line in the episode, 'I'm tried of being jabbed in the hand with a rip-off stick,' was a line that Bo Diddley had laid on me in about 1973 when I was writing a rock and roll column. I always thought it was a great line, and it was wonderful to work it into the script."

"High Dollar Bop"

Original Air Date 4/5/89
Written by Alfonse Ruggerio and John Schulian
Directed by Douglas Jackson
Guest Starring: Glenn Frey, Tim Curry, Pamela Segall, Paul McCrane, Paul Winfield, Patti D'Arbanville, Deirdre Hall, Billy Wirth and Ron Taylor

Nothing much happens in "High Dollar Bop," as the majority of the episode deals with Vinnie's attempts to get Johnny Medley and Monroe Blue to collaborate with Eddie Tempest, if they can get him out from under contract with Winston.

Wind of this conversation gets back to Winston, whose response is to have a couple of his men throw Medley off a roof, resulting in a broken back. At this point Vinnie realizes the full scope of what he's up against, and becomes more determined to take Newquay down.

During a high stakes card game, Isaac's gambling gets the best of him, and he actually loses Shakala records to Newquay. With the company goes Dead Dog Records, and thus Vinnie and Travis as well. Isaac actually seems delighted, because now he has the challenge of building a new company. Now he feels it's necessary to clear up the phony album debt owed to him, and it gives Frank the opportunity to arrest him as a willing participant in what is deemed a crime, as well as for tax evasion and other such activities. Frank eventually turns him to work for the government in a sting operation against Newquay.

The episode concludes with Vinnie deciding the game which cost Isaac his company was crooked.

Unfortunately, this episode seemed padded; its main elements could have been filtered into the show before and the one after.

"'High Dollar Bop' had Isaac Twine lose his company and Dead Dog Records in a crooked card game," John Schulian recalls. "We were put in touch with a guy known as a Card Protector, and all he does is go around to private games in hotel rooms and private homes, and makes sure they're on the up and up. So he gave us great material to use."

"Hip Hop on the Gravy Train"

Original Air Date 4/12/89
Written by Suzanne Oshry
Directed by Helaine Head
Guest Starring: Glenn Frey, Tim Curry, Paul Winfield, Patti D'Arbanville, Billy Wirth, Ken Jenkins and William L. Calhoun

Vinnie and the OCB put into effect a plan to make Newquay's life miserable, by informing Isaac the card game was crooked. And by arranging for a sting operation (the result being that he may get Shakala back) proving to Eddie Tempest that he and all of Radiance's acts have been ripped off and they are practically broke. They convince Claudia that as half owner of Radiance Records, she should have a more active role in the company's day-to-day operation.

Johnny Medley and wife

Being fully aware of Isaac's problems with the government, Amber arranges for Newquay to hire the two of them to run Shakala under the Radiance label, which delights Isaac. It will give him a chance to get even.

Later, Claudia, who's had another fight with Winston, finds solace in the arms of Eddie Tempest. In the midst of their lovemaking, they accidentally fall through a skylight to their death (and one has to admit that the method in which they fall seems contrived).

Another episode with a lot of problems. While it presents interesting elements, it is the second show in a row that seems to just fill time. Also, we lost Johnny Medley in "High Dollar Bop," and now we've lost Eddie Tempest and Claudia Newquay.

"The One That Got Away"

Original Air Date 5/3/89

Written by David J. Burke and Alfonse Ruggerio

Directed by Jorge Montesi

Guest Starring: Paul Winfield, Patti D'Arbanville, Glen Frey, Tim Curry, Mitchell Kosterman, Jeff Irvine and Ken Budd

Newquay has a court order delivered to Vinnie and Travis to have them expelled from the premises of Radiance Records, but Vinnie, who had been informed of the situation by the OCB, returns the favor with a cease and desist order which says they cannot be removed from the premises without just cause. As both orders are dated the same day, Newquay becomes suspicious and uses his government contacts to access Vinnie's file.

Angry at the treatment, Travis demands, as his contract guarantees, to have access to all aspects of Radiance Records. In response, Newquay makes him the company mail man, so that every piece of correspondence that arrives will pass through his hands first. At first Travis is enraged, but he realizes the benefit of the position and the full scope of information he can obtain. The one surprise he did not expect, however, is the package containing Vinnie's file, and the information that he is a cop. With panic, Vinnie takes Travis out of the building to a secluded area, where Travis relates how used and betrayed he feels. Vinnie apologizes, but emphasizes that what he knows can get him killed. Bobby swears he won't say anything, but if Vinnie does stay up all night worrying, then maybe they're even. Vinnie has to agree with that logic.

Travis makes his own power play, wondering if a deal could be made if Newquay can be brought down: specifically, he'd like Dead Dog Records. In return, he has a casette of "The Eddie Tempest Basement Tapes." The significance of this tape is that although Newquay owns everything that Tempest recorded, he doesn't own a "lick" of Monroe Blue, who is also on the tape. Vinnie wants to use the tape as a carrot, but Frank is concerned that it's entrapment, which will get them all thrown out of court.

Frank arrests Philip Kenderson, Newquay's government contact, and charges him with treason for shipping classified information. He will, however, be granted immunity if he cooperates. To that end, Kenderson meets with Newquay at a restaurant, saying that the information he needs on Terranova will cost money to grease the right hands. Newquay wants to know how much, but Kenderson asks him to make an offer. Suspecting something isn't right, Newquay orders Kenderson away. Then Newquay joins Isaac and Amber at another table, and is told about the Tempest cassette, which he listens to. He wants to know what the price is, and Isaac says he wants a piece of the overseas cleans operation that he has been running. Newquay admits (on tape, although he doesn't know it) that he's been making a fortune off of Tempest since his death, and that for the master tape he'll cut

Top: Diana Price (Debbie Harry) tries to avoid the controlling influences of Winston Newquay (Tim Curry)

Bottom: Amber Twine (Patti D'Arbanville) and her husband Isaac (Paul Winfield)

Isaac and Amber in. Money and the tape exchange hands, and the Feds move in to make an arrest.

The final scene shows Newquay in a jail cell, where his cellmate approaches him, apparently ready to inflict bodily harm. He recognizes him as Winston Newquay and breaks into an audition, as the two of them duet on "Soul Man."

"We were just kind of wobbling through the shows," says David Burke, "until we got to 'The One That Got Away,' where we started to resolve the whole situation, and that wonderful last scene where Winston Newquay is in jail and the guy sharing his cell starts auditioning for him. I love it!"

"Living and Dying in 4/4 Time"

Original Air Date 5/10/89

Written by Stephen Kronish and John Schulian

Directed by James Contner

Guest Starring: Paul Winfield, Patti D'Arbanville, Tim Curry, Ken Jenkins, Glenn Frey, Anthony J. Schembri, Stephen E. Miller, Lee Taylor, Rod Menzies and Christina Jastrzembska

As Frank feared, the Newquay case is thrown out of court due to entrapment, and everyone is back where they started. Back in his office, Newquay, feeling as though the walls are closing in around him, talks to a photo of Claudia, stating how much he really did love her even though they always fought.

Vinnie, not one to give up, comes up with the idea that Travis should eat away at Radiance from the inside, by calling up all of the label's acts and making them realize just how badly they've been ripped off. In between all this, Isaac, who's on the verge of getting Shakala Records back, suffers a heart attack and is brought to the hospital.

That night, Newquay visits Isaac and they make a wager that the first one who dies has to have the other one dance on his grave. They both laugh over the wager, and yet you know that they mean it with all their heart.

Next morning, Amber is back at the hospital. She and Isaac start kissing passionately, and he suffers a massive heart attack, and dies instantly. News of this reaches Newquay, who actually begins to cry, establishing a human element in him for the first time. We see that he and Isaac really did care for each other, despite their adversarial posturing.

Vinnie expresses his condolences to Amber, and as he leaves her building, he's surprised to find Newquay waiting for him in a limo. They reach the cemetery where Isaac is buried and Newquay asks Vinnie to become his business associate, as he finds a lot in him that he admires. Vinnie cannot return the favor, believing the collapse of Newquay's empire is something that he deserves, as would anyone who has spent a life crushing people. With no further words, Winston starts dancing on Isaac's grave. As he does so a smoke bomb is released, and Isaac's tape recorded voice says, "Got you, Winston....Forever and forever!"

"Indeed you did," cries Winston as he collapses beside the tombstone.

The arc comes to an end with Travis getting Dead Dog Records, Amber receiving Shakala, Newquay literally losing his mind and Vinnie establishing what eventually becomes an ongoing relationship with Amber.

Despite disappointments during the seven episodes, the music arc ended on a terrific note, as "Living and Dying in 4/4 Time" has wonderfully bizarre touches. Still, as most of the crew has stated, this arc went on too long and grew too large.

Diana Price (Debbie Harry) prepared to rehearse her first effort for Dead Dog Records

Diana Price (Debbie Harry) and Bobby Travis (Glenn Frey)

"This was the last episode of the arc," notes Stephen Kronish, "and by that time we had weeded out all of the other characters and were pretty much left to deal with Isaac and Winston, who were terrific in their performances. You saw these guys who were so adversarial, yet Winston could believably cry when Isaac died, because he was his only link to humanity. And that crazy bet they made about dancing on the grave, then to see Winston deteriorate into his weird Elvis thing. I'd known Tim from *The Rocky Horror Picture Show* and I said, 'We've got to get him to growl once in this arc,' which we did. You ended up feeling sorry for him, which is one of the nice things—to take some of these seemingly unsympathetic people and make them sympathetic."

John Schulian enthuses, "There was that great scene where Tim Curry dances on Isaac's grave and the grave blows up, which was my idea. I have to say that as much as I sit here and kvetch about David Burke, being in his presence and working with him inspires you to come up with scenes like that. David's a very, very talented guy."

Schulian, who was let go from **Wiseguy** at the conclusion of the second season, offers his opinion on what happened to the music arc and the show in general. "David Burke is really the force that shaped that show," he says. "Its strengths are his strengths, and the weaknesses are his weaknesses. He is not a planner. He flies by the seat of his pants, so what happens is you get a lot of steam up front in an arc, and then about mid-way through you tend to lose course, because he doesn't know where it's going to wind up. The way you write a script, at least most of the people I know—Bochco, Tarses, Dick Wolf—sit down and know where you're going to wind up. You know where each act break is and how things are going to end up. We never did that when we wrote an arc, and we never knew where we were going. When he sits down to do the script, you'd work your way through the first three acts and he'd say, 'Ah, the fourth act will write itself.' So there is a lot of that, not putting the ribbon on the package, although he kind of knows where he's going. Now let's talk about the rock and roll arc, which was an abysmal failure. I am probably the guy who lobbied the hardest for us to do it. You talk about an arc petering out...."

"I was very disappointed with the music arc," he continues, "and it sort of guaranteed that I wouldn't be back on the show for its third year. It proved that Burke, Kronish and I were on different wavelengths. For instance, one of the things David and I disagreed on is that he didn't think you need guns to create tension, and I agree with him up to a point. But this is the world Vinnie lives in, and you've got to have them or you're cheating. Two people dressed in nice suits and screaming at each other isn't my idea of entertainment."

Robert Iscove, who did not direct any episodes of the music arc, observes, "What *is* the problem in the music arc? Is there a CD that's going to blow up? Payola? It's so hard to sustain why the OCB is involved. It was the only arc that really didn't work, and what happened is that they had so much success with stars like Jerry Lewis and Ron Silver, that they went a little crazy with them. They had so many people to deal with, that there just wasn't enough time to write them good scenes in every episode. It didn't hold together as well as the other arcs, because then you only had one or two bad guys that you followed."

He's quick to add, however, that **Wiseguy** is a show he loves to work on, and that David Burke is someone he enjoys working with.

"David gives me the hard stuff," he says, "and I keep saying, 'Give me harder stuff,' so we keep pushing each other in that way. He'll back off on something and I'll say, 'No, I can do that.' I know I can go a little nuts, as long as I have great writing and great scenes to come back to. Of all the television I've done, this is the most interesting because the characters within the scenes live. I like doing the shows that have more action in them, because to me the success of **Wiseguy** is the action with the emotional drama. A pure action show would be terrible, and two heads in a room talking would be dull. I like the guys who do the show a lot."

SEASON TWO CAMPING TRIP

"Call It Casaba"
Original Air Date 5/17/89
Written by Clifton Campbell, Alfonse Ruggerio and David J. Burke
Directed by Gus Trikonis
Guest Starring: Patti D'Arbanville, Lisa Waltz, Barry Greene, Coletta Wise and Peter Anderson

A change of pace episode, "Call It Casaba" deals with Vinnie, Frank and Lifeguard (a.k.a. Uncle Mike, a.k.a. Daniel Benjamin Burroughs) going off on a camping trip to a cabin that is owned by Lifeguard. There they try to have a good time while off duty, but each is experiencing a different problem. Lifeguard is trying to come to grips with his relationship with his daughter. Now she's getting married and he doesn't know if he'll fit into her life at all, although he wants to. Frank is morose over the way his marriage fell apart and how he doesn't know what the next step should be, and Vinnie discusses the isolation he feels working with the OCB, going through life with people thinking he's a mobster.

The episode concludes with Lifeguard spending time with his daughter, Frank calling Jenny for dinner and Vinnie getting in touch with Amber Twine, and asking her for a date.

Probably the most enjoyable aspect of this episode was that it gave us the opportunity to see the three main leads interacting outside of work.

"After the music arc," offers David Burke, "the rest of the year was just an attempt to get through the season. 'Casaba' was satisfying to us. It was really a nice episode and it brought our three main characters down to a more human level."

Frank McPike (Jonathan Banks) is not a happy camper

126

SEASON TWO
FINALE

"Le Lacrime de L'Amour"

Original Air Date 5/24/89

Part 1 Written by Suzanne Oshry and John Schulian

Part 1 Directed by Frank Johnson

Part 2 Written by Alfonse Ruggerio and Clifton Campbell

Part 2 Directed by Bill Corcoran

Guest Starring: Patti D'Arbanville, Elsa Raven, George O. Petrie, Robert Davi, Patricia Harty, Mike Starr, Thomas Ian Griffin, Mimi Lieber, John Snyder, Richard Sarafian and Tony Romano

Part one deals primarily with the attempts of Amber's lawyer to get her to sell Shakala Records. Vinnie believes his intent is less than honest, but she chalks his feelings up to jealousy, although Vinnie himself can't tell if that's the problem. He's not sure whether he's falling for her or not. Ultimately it turns out that he's right, her lawyer is representing a company eager to purchase her property for its real estate value.

Part two shows that the relationship between Vinnie and Amber has developed, the two are falling very much in love. Carlotta and don Aiuppo hear that there's a woman in his life, and come back to Brooklyn from their trip to the old country. Upon their arrival, Carlotta becomes very judgmental, feeling that Amber is not right for her son, although these feelings are ultimately worked out.

Meanwhile, Aiuppo meets with the various mob families, explaining to them that Vinnie is his son, but that in no way does this signify his torch of power being passed down. Vincenzo is not in la familia, but should anybody harm him, Aiuppo himself will return to the business, "and that is something you do not want."

At episode's conclusion, an assassination attempt is made on Aiuppo's life, when he is struck down in his greenhouse by machinegun fire.

"The whole first part of the two part finale read like an episode of *Thirtysomething*," says John Schulian. "It was about relationships, and nobody watches **Wiseguy** to see relationships and whiny, yuppie crap. That's the way it turned out. I hated that episode with a passion, but I loved the Don Aiuppo half because I think George Petrie is a fine actor."

David Burke adds, "Part of it worked, but it was also problematic because it started out as two individual hours and the network decided they wanted to put them together, even though they had nothing to do with each other. We had to figure out how to do it and it was a race to do so. The stuff with Don Aiuppo worked for me. The last hour worked better than the first hour. The setting up of the first arc of the third year also worked for me, but there was just no way for those two episodes to go together."

CONCLUSIONS

And thus **Wiseguy**'s second season ended on a considerably less positive note than the first year, and yet somehow it still stood above the standard fare found on prime time television. If one particular complaint can be addressed to the show, it's that the viewer never really felt the connection between Vinnie and one of his adversaries in the same way it was felt for Sonny Steelgrave. By the same token, David Burke was probably right when he said that no matter what they did, there was simply no way to equal that first arc.

"The second season was not as good as the first season," he concedes. "The bottom line is because Ken Wahl was crippled, which caused us to redo everything and we fell apart towards the end of the year because we were so exhausted. It's just a natural thing for television anyway. Conversely, I think the garment arc is the best we've done, and those shows along with 'Stairway to Heaven', 'White Noise' and 'Dead Dog Lives' in some ways exceeded the first year in that we demonstrated a much deeper range, which was important."

While everyone connected with the show believes they're doing their best work, they all would love to see it pay off in higher ratings, although no one dwells on the subject.

"We really do believe there's an audience out there that would love the show, if they would just give us a shot," points out Les Sheldon. "But let's face it, we're never going to be a number one show. We're not *Cosby*. There are a lot of shows on the air that are entertaining in their own way. I don't believe in good or bad. We have a show that entertains in the direction we entertain in, and we're not going to hit a home run with everybody. We are conscious that we're in the business to entertain, so we're not self-indulgent in that way. That's one of the joys of working with these people. It's tough, but I know at the end there's a rainbow. We all lean on each other, we fully collaborate with Ken and he with us, and it's a joy. As far as where we want to go, we just want to keep on keeping on. Even if we were to get canceled, it wouldn't be a bad moment, because every moment we were fortunate to work on this show was worth it."

David Burke concurs. "I have done things on this show that Michael Mann would not let me do on *Crime Story*," he says. "I've taken notions into Cannell at which he's raised an eyebrow, but has said, 'If you believe in it, go do it.' Steve is a writer, and he understands the joy of pushing at the envelope a little bit and trying to make things play. It's a thrill to be a part. If we're doing quality here—if that's what it's deemed—then it's because Steve Cannell has allowed it to happen. I have been in other places where executives interfere with it happening, or are too busy trying to please marketing research and network notes, as opposed to building a good foundation from the get-go. I've seen friends of mine who are writers/producers, frustrated at the experience of having shows that did not reflect their true talents. There are television shows that don't have quality, and to them I would have to raise an eyebrow towards the executive suite,

129

because there are a lot of people out there doing shows that are very good, but are hemmed in. I feel like I have found a good home here.

"I wish I could come up with some magic enticement for the audience," Burke closes. "We've done fairly well in the ratings and my feeling is that you can't beat the drum for thoughtful television and then not watch it, and nonetheless expect it to be there."

Wiseguy remains thoughtful television, combining suspense, action and—most importantly—riveting characterization in a unique blend that is completely unlike any other series on the air.

Ken Wahl ready for the third season as WISEGUY Vinnie Terranova

THE MAKING OF A WISEGUY

The Phantom
The Green Hornet
The Shadow
The Batman

Each issue of Serials Adventures Presents offers 100 or more pages of pure nostalgic fun for $16.95

SERIALS ADVENTURES MAGAZINE

Flash Gordon Part One
Flash Gordon Part Two
Blackhawk

Each issue of Serials Adventures Presents features a chapter by chapter review of a rare serial combined with biographies of the stars and behind-the-scenes information. Plus rare photos. See the videotapes and read the books!

UNCLE

THE U.N.C.L.E. TECHNICAL MANUAL

Every technical device completely detailed and blueprinted, including weapons, communications, weaponry, organization, facitilites... 80 pages. 2 volumes...$9.95 each

PRISONER

NUMBER SIX: THE COMPLEAT PRISONER

The most unique and intelligent television series ever aired! Patrick McGoohan's tour-de-force of spies and mental mazes finally explained episode by episode, including an interview with the McGoohan and the complete layout of the real village!...160 pages...$14.95

GREEN HORNET TELEVISION

THE GREEN HORNET

Daring action adventure with the Green Hornet and Kato. This show appeared before Bruce Lee had achieved popularity but delivered fun, superheroic action. Episode guide and character profiles combine to tell the whole story...120 pages...$14.95

WILD, WILD, WEST

WILD, WILD, WEST

Is it a Western or a Spy show? We couldn't decide so we're listing it twice. Fantastic adventure, convoluted plots, incredible devices...all set in the wild, wild west! Details of fantastic devices, character profiles and an episode-by-episode guide...120 pages...$17.95

THE FREDDY KRUEGER STORY

The making of the monster. Including interviews with director Wes Craven and star Robert Englund. Plus an interview with Freddy himself!
$14.95

THE ALIENS STORY

Interviews with movie director James Cameron, stars Sigourney Weaver and Michael Biehn and effects people and designers Ron Cobb, Syd Mead, Doug Beswick and lots more!...$14.95

ROBOCOP

Law enforcement in the future. Includes interviews with the stars, the director, the writer, the special effects people, the storyboard artists and the makeup men! $16.95

MONSTERLAND'S HORROR IN THE '80s

The definitive book of the horror films of the '80s. Includes interviews with the stars and makers of Aliens, Freddy Krueger, Robocop, Predator, Fright Night, Terminator and all the others! $17.95

LOST IN SPACE

THE COMPLEAT LOST IN SPACE

244 PAGES...$17.95

TRIBUTE BOOK

Interviews with everyone!...$7.95

TECH MANUAL

Technical diagrams to all of the special ships and devices plus exclusive production artwork....$9.95

GERRY ANDERSON

SUPERMARIONATION

Episode guides and character profiles to Capt Scarlet, Stingray, Fireball, Thunderbirds, Supercar and more...240 pages...$17.95

BEAUTY AND THE BEAST

THE UNOFFICIAL BEAUTY&BEAST

Complete first season guide including interviews and biographies of the stars.
132 pages
$14.95

DARK SHADOWS

DARK SHADOWS TRIBUTE BOOK

Interviews, scripts and more...
160 pages...$14.95

DARK SHADOWS INTERVIEWS BOOK

A special book interviewing the entire cast.
$18.95

DOCTOR WHO THE BAKER YEARS

A complete guide to Tom Baker's seasons as the Doctor including an in-depth episode guide, interviews with the companions and profiles of the characters...
300 pages...$19.95

THE DOCTOR WHO ENCYCLOPEDIA: THE FOURTH DOCTOR

Encyclopedia of every character, villain and monster of the Baker Years.
..240 pages...$19.95

Boring, but Necessary Ordering Information!

Payment: All orders must be prepaid by check or money order. Do not send cash. All payments must be made in US funds only.

Shipping: We offer several methods of shipment for our product.

Postage is as follows:

For books priced under $10.00— for the first book add $2.50. For each additional book under $10.00 add $1.00. (This is per individual book priced under $10.00, not the order total.)

For books priced over $10.00— for the first book add $3.25. For each additional book over $10.00 add $2.00. (This is per individual book priced over $10.00, not the order total.)

These orders are filled as quickly as possible. Sometimes a book can be delayed if we are temporarily out of stock. You should note on your order whether you prefer us to ship the book as soon as available or send you a merchandise credit good for other TV goodies or send you your money back immediately. Shipments normally take 2 or 3 weeks, but allow up to 12 weeks for delivery.

Special UPS 2 Day Blue Label RUSH SERVICE: Special service is available for desperate Couch Potatos. These books are shipped within 24 hours of when we receive your order and should take 2 days to get from us to you.

For the first **RUSH SERVICE** book under $10.00 add $4.00. For each additional 1 book under $10.00 and $1.25. (This is per individual book priced under $10.00, not the order total.)

For the first **RUSH SERVICE** book over $10.00 add $6.00. For each additional book over $10.00 add $3.50 per book. (This is per individual book priced over $10.00, not the order total.)

Canadian and Foreign shipping rates are the same except that Blue Label RUSH SERVICE is not available. All Canadian and Foreign orders are shipped as books or printed matter.

DISCOUNTS! DISCOUNTS! Because your orders are what keep us in business we offer a discount to people that buy a lot of our books as our way of saying thanks. On orders over $25.00 we give a 5% discount. On orders over $50.00 we give a 10% discount. On orders over $100.00 we give a 15% discount. On orders over $150.00 we give a 20% discount. Please list alternates when possible. Please state if you wish a refund or for us to backorder an item if it is not in stock.

100% satisfaction guaranteed. We value your support. You will receive a full refund as long as the copy of the book you are not happy with is received back by us in reasonable condition. No questions asked, except we would like to know how we failed you. Refunds and credits are given as soon as we receive back the item you do not want.

Please have mercy on Phyllis and carefully fill out this form in the neatest way you can. Remember, she has to read a lot of them every day and she wants to get it right and keep you happy! You may use a duplicate of this order blank as long as it is clear. **Please don't forget to include payment! And remember, we** *love* **repeat friends...**

■■■■■■■■■■■■■■■■■■■■■■■■■■■■**ORDER FORM**■■■■■■■■■■■■■■■■■■■■■■■■■■■■

_____The Phantom $16.95
_____The Green Hornet $16.95
_____The Shadow $16.95
_____Flash Gordon Part One $16.95 _____Part Two $16.95
_____Blackhawk $16.95
_____Batman $16.95
_____The UNCLE Technical Manual One $9.95 _____Two $9.95
_____The Green Hornet Television Book $14.95
_____Number Six The Prisoner Book $14.95
_____The Wild Wild West $17.95
_____Trek Year One $10.95
_____Trek Year Two $12.95
_____Trek Year Three $12.95
_____The Animated Trek $14.95
_____The Movies $12.95
_____Next Generation $19.95
_____The Lost Years $14.95
_____The Trek Encyclopedia $19.95
_____Interviews Aboard The Enterprise $18.95
_____The Ultimate Trek $75.00
_____Trek Handbook $12.95 _____Trek Universe $17.95
_____The Crew Book $17.95
_____The Making of the Next Generation $14.95
_____The Freddy Krueger Story $14.95
_____The Aliens Story $14.95
_____Robocop $16.95
_____Monsterland's Horror in the '80s $17.95
_____The Compleat Lost in Space $17.95
_____Lost in Space Tribute Book $9.95
_____Lost in Space Tech Manual $9.95
_____Supermarionation $17.95
_____The Unofficial Beauty and the Beast $14.95
_____Dark Shadows Tribute Book $14.95
_____Dark Shadows Interview Book $18.95
_____Doctor Who Baker Years $19.95
_____The Doctor Who Encyclopedia: The 4th Doctor $19.95
_____Illustrated Stephen King $12.95
_____Gunsmoke Years $14.95

NAME:_____

STREET:_____

CITY:_____

STATE:_____

ZIP:_____

TOTAL:_____ SHIPPING_____

SEND TO: COUCH POTATO, INC.
5715 N BALSAM, LAS VEGAS, NV 89130

EXCITING EARLY ISSUES!

If your local comic book specialty store no longer has copies of the early issues you may want to order them directly from us.

By Roy Crane:
_Buz Sawyer #1 _Buz Sawyer #2 _Buz Sawyer #3 _Buz Sawyer #4 _Buz Sawyer #5

By Alex Raymond:
_Jungle Jim 1_Jungle Jim 2_Jungle Jim 3_Jungle Jim 4 _Jungle Jim 5 _Jungle Jim 6 _Jungle Jim 7
_Rip Kirby #1_Rip Kirby #2 _Rip Kirby #3 _Rip Kirby #4

By Lee Falk and Phil Davis:
_Mandrake #1_Mandrake #2_Mandrake #3 _Mandrake #4 _Mandrake #5 _Mandrake #6 _Mandrake #7

By Peter O'Donnell and Jim Holdaway:
_Modesty1 _Modesty 2_Modesty 3 _Modesty 4_Modesty 5 _Modesty#6 _Modesty#7 _Modesty ANNUAL ($5.00)

By Hal Foster:
_P V #1 _P V #2 _P V #3 _P V #4 _P V #5 _P V #6 _P V #7 _P V #8 _P V AN. ($5.00)

By Archie Goodwin and Al Williamson:
_Secret Agent #1 _Secret Agent #2_Secret Agent #3 _Secret Agent #4 _Secret Agent #5 _Secret Agent #6

(All about the heroes including interviews with Hal Foster, Lee Falk and Al Williamson:)
___ THE KING COMIC HEROES $14.95
(The following two book-size collections preserve the original strip format)
___ THE MANDRAKE SUNDAYS $14.95
___ **THE PHANTOM SUNDAYS $14.95**

___ (Enclosed) Please enclose $3.00 per comic ordered
and/or $17.95 for THE KING COMIC HEROES
and/or $14.95 for THE MANDRAKE SUNDAYS.
and/or $14.95 for THE PHANTOM SUNDAYS.
Shipping and handling are included.

Name: _ _ _ _ _ _ _ _ _ _ _ _ _ _

Street: _ _ _ _ _ _ _ _ _ _ _ _ _ _

City: _ _ _ _ _ _ _ _ _ _ _ _ _ _ _ _

State: _ _ _ _ _ _ _ _ _ _ _ _ _ _ _

Zip   Code: _ _ _ _ _ _ _ _ _ _ _
Check or money order only. No cash please. All payments must be in US funds. Please add $5.00 to foreign orders.
I remembered to enclose:$_____
Please send to:
Pioneer, 5715 N. Balsam Rd., Las Vegas, NV 89130